Hybrid Sharepoint
Complete Self-Assessme

The guidance in this Self-Assessm... ....d on Hybrid Sharepoint best practices and standards in business process architecture, design and quality management. The guidance is also based on the professional judgment of the individual collaborators listed in the Acknowledgments.

Notice of rights

You are licensed to use the Self-Assessment contents in your presentations and materials for internal use and customers without asking us - we are here to help.

All rights reserved for the book itself: this book may not be reproduced or transmitted in any form by any means, electronic, mechanical, photocopying, recording, or otherwise, without the prior written permission of the publisher.

The information in this book is distributed on an "As Is" basis without warranty. While every precaution has been taken in the preparation of he book, neither the author nor the publisher shall have any liability to any person or entity with respect to any loss or damage caused or alleged to be caused directly or indirectly by the instructions contained in this book or by the products described in it.

Trademarks

Many of the designations used by manufacturers and sellers to distinguish their products are claimed as trademarks. Where those designations appear in this book, and the publisher was aware of a trademark claim, the designations appear as requested by the owner of the trademark. All other product names and services identified throughout this book are used in editorial fashion only and for the benefit of such companies with no intention of infringement of the trademark. No such use, or the use of any trade name, is intended to convey endorsement or other affiliation with this book.

Copyright © by The Art of Service
http://theartofservice.com
service@theartofservice.com

Table of Contents

About The Art of Service	7
Acknowledgments	8
Included Resources - how to access	9
Your feedback is invaluable to us	11
Purpose of this Self-Assessment	11
How to use the Self-Assessment	12
Hybrid Sharepoint Scorecard Example	14
Hybrid Sharepoint Scorecard	15
BEGINNING OF THE SELF-ASSESSMENT:	16
CRITERION #1: RECOGNIZE	17
CRITERION #2: DEFINE:	25
CRITERION #3: MEASURE:	36
CRITERION #4: ANALYZE:	43
CRITERION #5: IMPROVE:	58
CRITERION #6: CONTROL:	68
CRITERION #7: SUSTAIN:	77
Hybrid Sharepoint and Managing Projects, Criteria for Project Managers:	125
1.0 Initiating Process Group: Hybrid Sharepoint	126
1.1 Project Charter: Hybrid Sharepoint	128
1.2 Stakeholder Register: Hybrid Sharepoint	130

1.3 Stakeholder Analysis Matrix: Hybrid Sharepoint — 131

2.0 Planning Process Group: Hybrid Sharepoint — 133

2.1 Project Management Plan: Hybrid Sharepoint — 135

2.2 Scope Management Plan: Hybrid Sharepoint — 137

2.3 Requirements Management Plan: Hybrid Sharepoint — 139

2.4 Requirements Documentation: Hybrid Sharepoint — 141

2.5 Requirements Traceability Matrix: Hybrid Sharepoint — 143

2.6 Project Scope Statement: Hybrid Sharepoint — 145

2.7 Assumption and Constraint Log: Hybrid Sharepoint — 147

2.8 Work Breakdown Structure: Hybrid Sharepoint — 149

2.9 WBS Dictionary: Hybrid Sharepoint — 151

2.10 Schedule Management Plan: Hybrid Sharepoint — 153

2.11 Activity List: Hybrid Sharepoint — 155

2.12 Activity Attributes: Hybrid Sharepoint — 157

2.13 Milestone List: Hybrid Sharepoint — 159

2.14 Network Diagram: Hybrid Sharepoint — 161

2.15 Activity Resource Requirements: Hybrid Sharepoint — 163

2.16 Resource Breakdown Structure: Hybrid Sharepoint — 165

2.17 Activity Duration Estimates: Hybrid Sharepoint — 167

2.18 Duration Estimating Worksheet: Hybrid Sharepoint 169

2.19 Project Schedule: Hybrid Sharepoint 171

2.20 Cost Management Plan: Hybrid Sharepoint 173

2.21 Activity Cost Estimates: Hybrid Sharepoint 175

2.22 Cost Estimating Worksheet: Hybrid Sharepoint 177

2.23 Cost Baseline: Hybrid Sharepoint 179

2.24 Quality Management Plan: Hybrid Sharepoint 181

2.25 Quality Metrics: Hybrid Sharepoint 183

2.26 Process Improvement Plan: Hybrid Sharepoint 185

2.27 Responsibility Assignment Matrix: Hybrid Sharepoint 187

2.28 Roles and Responsibilities: Hybrid Sharepoint 189

2.29 Human Resource Management Plan: Hybrid Sharepoint 191

2.30 Communications Management Plan: Hybrid Sharepoint 193

2.31 Risk Management Plan: Hybrid Sharepoint 195

2.32 Risk Register: Hybrid Sharepoint 197

2.33 Probability and Impact Assessment: Hybrid Sharepoint 199

2.34 Probability and Impact Matrix: Hybrid Sharepoint 201

2.35 Risk Data Sheet: Hybrid Sharepoint   203

2.36 Procurement Management Plan: Hybrid Sharepoint   205

2.37 Source Selection Criteria: Hybrid Sharepoint   207

2.38 Stakeholder Management Plan: Hybrid Sharepoint   209

2.39 Change Management Plan: Hybrid Sharepoint   211

3.0 Executing Process Group: Hybrid Sharepoint   213

3.1 Team Member Status Report: Hybrid Sharepoint   215

3.2 Change Request: Hybrid Sharepoint   217

3.3 Change Log: Hybrid Sharepoint   219

3.4 Decision Log: Hybrid Sharepoint   221

3.5 Quality Audit: Hybrid Sharepoint   223

3.6 Team Directory: Hybrid Sharepoint   226

3.7 Team Operating Agreement: Hybrid Sharepoint   228

3.8 Team Performance Assessment: Hybrid Sharepoint   230

3.9 Team Member Performance Assessment: Hybrid Sharepoint   232

3.10 Issue Log: Hybrid Sharepoint   234

4.0 Monitoring and Controlling Process Group: Hybrid Sharepoint   236

4.1 Project Performance Report: Hybrid Sharepoint   238

4.2 Variance Analysis: Hybrid Sharepoint   240

4.3 Earned Value Status: Hybrid Sharepoint   242

4.4 Risk Audit: Hybrid Sharepoint   244

4.5 Contractor Status Report: Hybrid Sharepoint   246

4.6 Formal Acceptance: Hybrid Sharepoint   248

5.0 Closing Process Group: Hybrid Sharepoint   250

5.1 Procurement Audit: Hybrid Sharepoint   252

5.2 Contract Close-Out: Hybrid Sharepoint   254

5.3 Project or Phase Close-Out: Hybrid Sharepoint   256

5.4 Lessons Learned: Hybrid Sharepoint   258
Index   260

About The Art of Service

The Art of Service, Business Process Architects since 2000, is dedicated to helping stakeholders achieve excellence.

Defining, designing, creating, and implementing a process to solve a stakeholders challenge or meet an objective is the most valuable role... In EVERY group, company, organization and department.

Unless you're talking a one-time, single-use project, there should be a process. Whether that process is managed and implemented by humans, AI, or a combination of the two, it needs to be designed by someone with a complex enough perspective to ask the right questions.

Someone capable of asking the right questions and step back and say, 'What are we really trying to accomplish here? And is there a different way to look at it?'

With The Art of Service's Standard Requirements Self-Assessments, we empower people who can do just that — whether their title is marketer, entrepreneur, manager, salesperson, consultant, Business Process Manager, executive assistant, IT Manager, CIO etc... —they are the people who rule the future. They are people who watch the process as it happens, and ask the right questions to make the process work better.

Contact us when you need any support with this Self-Assessment and any help with templates, blue-prints and examples of standard documents you might need:

http://theartofservice.com
service@theartofservice.com

Acknowledgments

This checklist was developed under the auspices of The Art of Service, chaired by Gerardus Blokdyk.

Representatives from several client companies participated in the preparation of this Self-Assessment.

In addition, we are thankful for the design and printing services provided.

Included Resources - how to access

Included with your purchase of the book is the Hybrid Sharepoint Self-Assessment Spreadsheet Dashboard which contains all questions and Self-Assessment areas and auto-generates insights, graphs, and project RACI planning - all with examples to get you started right away.

How? Simply send an email to
access@theartofservice.com
with this books' title in the subject to get the Hybrid Sharepoint Self Assessment Tool right away.

You will receive the following contents with New and Updated specific criteria:

- The latest quick edition of the book in PDF

- The latest complete edition of the book in PDF, which criteria correspond to the criteria in...

- The Self-Assessment Excel Dashboard, and...

- Example pre-filled Self-Assessment Excel Dashboard to get familiar with results generation

- In-depth specific Checklists covering the topic

- Project management checklists and templates to assist with implementation

INCLUDES LIFETIME SELF ASSESSMENT UPDATES

Every self assessment comes with Lifetime Updates and Lifetime Free Updated Books. Lifetime Updates is an industry-first feature which allows you to receive verified self assessment updates, ensuring you always have the most accurate information at your fingertips.

Get it now- you will be glad you did - do it now, before you forget.

Send an email to **access@theartofservice.com** with this books' title in the subject to get the Hybrid Sharepoint Self Assessment Tool right away.

Your feedback is invaluable to us

If you recently bought this book, we would love to hear from you! You can do this by writing a review on amazon (or the online store where you purchased this book) about your last purchase! As part of our continual service improvement process, we love to hear real client experiences and feedback.

How does it work?
To post a review on Amazon, just log in to your account and click on the Create Your Own Review button (under Customer Reviews) of the relevant product page. You can find examples of product reviews in Amazon. If you purchased from another online store, simply follow their procedures.

What happens when I submit my review?
Once you have submitted your review, send us an email at review@theartofservice.com with the link to your review so we can properly thank you for your feedback.

Purpose of this Self-Assessment

This Self-Assessment has been developed to improve understanding of the requirements and elements of Hybrid Sharepoint, based on best practices and standards in business process architecture, design and quality management.

It is designed to allow for a rapid Self-Assessment to determine how closely existing management practices and procedures correspond to the elements of the Self-Assessment.

The criteria of requirements and elements of Hybrid Sharepoint have been rephrased in the format of a Self-Assessment questionnaire, with a seven-criterion scoring system, as explained in this document.

In this format, even with limited background knowledge of Hybrid

Sharepoint, a manager can quickly review existing operations to determine how they measure up to the standards. This in turn can serve as the starting point of a 'gap analysis' to identify management tools or system elements that might usefully be implemented in the organization to help improve overall performance.

How to use the Self-Assessment

On the following pages are a series of questions to identify to what extent your Hybrid Sharepoint initiative is complete in comparison to the requirements set in standards.

To facilitate answering the questions, there is a space in front of each question to enter a score on a scale of '1' to '5'.

1 Strongly Disagree

2 Disagree

3 Neutral

4 Agree

5 Strongly Agree

Read the question and rate it with the following in front of mind:

'In my belief, the answer to this question is clearly defined'.

There are two ways in which you can choose to interpret this statement;
1. how aware are you that the answer to the question is clearly defined
2. for more in-depth analysis you can choose to gather

evidence and confirm the answer to the question. This obviously will take more time, most Self-Assessment users opt for the first way to interpret the question and dig deeper later on based on the outcome of the overall Self-Assessment.

A score of '1' would mean that the answer is not clear at all, where a '5' would mean the answer is crystal clear and defined. Leave emtpy when the question is not applicable or you don't want to answer it, you can skip it without affecting your score. Write your score in the space provided.

After you have responded to all the appropriate statements in each section, compute your average score for that section, using the formula provided, and round to the nearest tenth. Then transfer to the corresponding spoke in the Hybrid Sharepoint Scorecard on the second next page of the Self-Assessment.

Your completed Hybrid Sharepoint Scorecard will give you a clear presentation of which Hybrid Sharepoint areas need attention.

Hybrid Sharepoint Scorecard Example

Example of how the finalized Scorecard can look like:

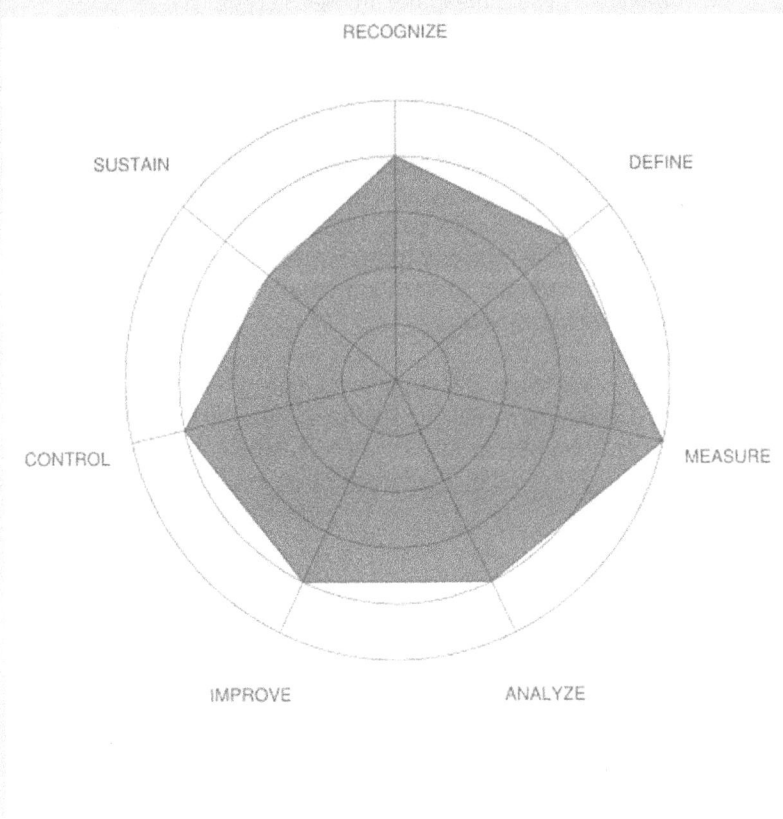

Hybrid Sharepoint Scorecard

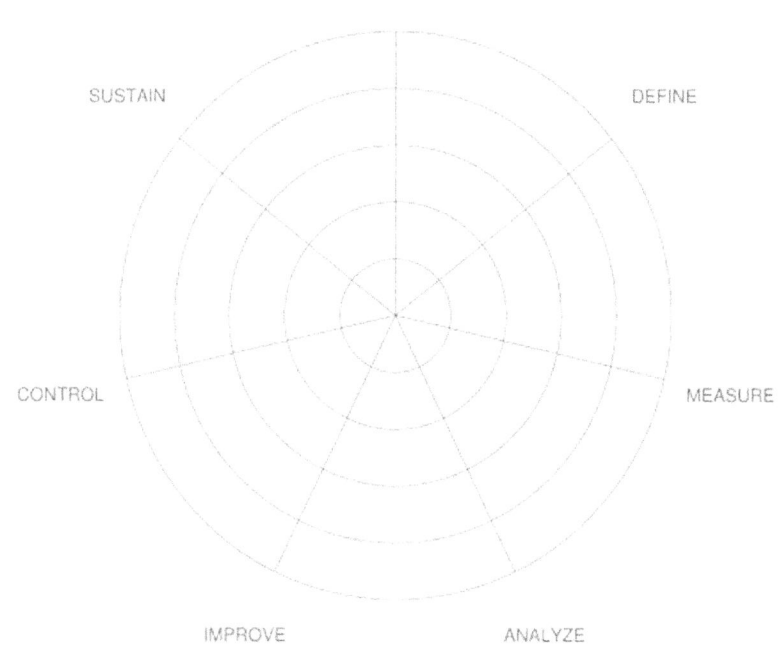

BEGINNING OF THE SELF-ASSESSMENT:

CRITERION #1: RECOGNIZE

INTENT: Be aware of the need for change. Recognize that there is an unfavorable variation, problem or symptom.

In my belief, the answer to this question is clearly defined:

5 Strongly Agree

4 Agree

3 Neutral

2 Disagree

1 Strongly Disagree

1. How do you stay flexible and focused to recognize larger Hybrid Sharepoint results?
<--- Score

2. To what extent does management recognize Hybrid Sharepoint as a tool to increase the results?
<--- Score

3. What do you need to do if you want a SharePoint

site?
<--- Score

4. Are adjustments needed for discovery tools to provide inventory and other controls across hybrid environments?
<--- Score

5. What does it need from systems management?
<--- Score

6. Does the service do what you need?
<--- Score

7. Network configuration and latency: do you need to change the network configuration to satisfy the latency requirements of an application in the cloud?
<--- Score

8. What situation(s) led to this Hybrid Sharepoint Self Assessment?
<--- Score

9. What skills need to be retained?
<--- Score

10. Do you need a cloud architect?
<--- Score

11. Can your application prevent concurrent logins?
<--- Score

**12. Are employees recognized or rewarded for performance that demonstrates the highest levels

of integrity?
<--- Score

13. Are there any specific expectations or concerns about the Hybrid Sharepoint team, Hybrid Sharepoint itself?
<--- Score

14. Is the need for organizational change recognized?
<--- Score

15. How are you going to measure success?
<--- Score

16. What business need are you addressing?
<--- Score

17. Do you need to consider hybrid implementation?
<--- Score

18. What are the stakeholder objectives to be achieved with Hybrid Sharepoint?
<--- Score

19. Are there recognized Hybrid Sharepoint problems?
<--- Score

20. How do you prevent unintentional cloud administration errors?
<--- Score

21. What structures need to be in place to deliver value?

<--- Score

22. What are the minority interests and what amount of minority interests can be recognized?
<--- Score

23. How do they identify the right platform for migration?
<--- Score

24. Does Hybrid Sharepoint create potential expectations in other areas that need to be recognized and considered?
<--- Score

25. As a sponsor, customer or management, how important is it to meet goals, objectives?
<--- Score

26. What problems are you facing and how do you consider Hybrid Sharepoint will circumvent those obstacles?
<--- Score

27. To what extent does each concerned units management team recognize Hybrid Sharepoint as an effective investment?
<--- Score

28. Are all the interfaces identified?
<--- Score

29. What do you need the system to do?
<--- Score

30. Do you need to use sharepoint designer?

<--- Score

31. Are Hybrid Sharepoint changes recognized early enough to be approved through the regular process?
<--- Score

32. What problems does cloud computing solve?
<--- Score

33. Will a response program recognize when a crisis occurs and provide some level of response?
<--- Score

34. Can management personnel recognize the monetary benefit of Hybrid Sharepoint?
<--- Score

35. How do you support DevOps needs for speed and agility?
<--- Score

36. What are the expected benefits of Hybrid Sharepoint to the stakeholder?
<--- Score

37. What business problem are you trying to solve ?
<--- Score

38. Which CSP services do you need?
<--- Score

39. What do you need for hybrid?
<--- Score

40. How are the Hybrid Sharepoint's objectives aligned to the group's overall stakeholder strategy?
<--- Score

41. What would happen if Hybrid Sharepoint weren't done?
<--- Score

42. What practices helps your organization to develop its capacity to recognize patterns?
<--- Score

43. How much are sponsors, customers, partners, stakeholders involved in Hybrid Sharepoint? In other words, what are the risks, if Hybrid Sharepoint does not deliver successfully?
<--- Score

44. What job skills do you think you will need for the future IT work environment?
<--- Score

45. When a Hybrid Sharepoint manager recognizes a problem, what options are available?
<--- Score

46. Are controls defined to recognize and contain problems?
<--- Score

47. Does your organization really need Slack, Jabber, Jive, and Microsoft Teams?
<--- Score

48. What happens when Google has a problem or goes down?

<--- Score

49. Have all project stakeholders been identified?
<--- Score

50. Do applications need to be modified?
<--- Score

51. Do you need it to authenticate users?
<--- Score

52. Do you need local storage as well as cloud storage?
<--- Score

53. Can you get it out if you need to?
<--- Score

54. When do you need a Hybrid DMZ?
<--- Score

55. Do you need to upgrade any mail servers?
<--- Score

56. Who else hopes to benefit from it?
<--- Score

57. How can you prevent your organization from becoming the next victim of a major cyber attack?
<--- Score

58. What dependencies need to be solved?
<--- Score

59. To what extent would your organization benefit from being recognized as a award

recipient?
<--- Score

60. How do you remove a SharePoint site that is no longer needed?
<--- Score

61. Who has and needs access to what?
<--- Score

62. Should you invest in industry-recognized qualifications?
<--- Score

63. What does Hybrid Sharepoint success mean to the stakeholders?
<--- Score

Add up total points for this section:
_____ = Total points for this section

Divided by: _____ (number of statements answered) = _____
Average score for this section

Transfer your score to the Hybrid Sharepoint Index at the beginning of the Self-Assessment.

CRITERION #2: DEFINE:

INTENT: Formulate the stakeholder problem. Define the problem, needs and objectives.

In my belief, the answer to this question is clearly defined:

5 Strongly Agree

4 Agree

3 Neutral

2 Disagree

1 Strongly Disagree

1. Has/have the customer(s) been identified?
<--- Score

2. Is data collected and displayed to better understand customer(s) critical needs and requirements.
<--- Score

3. Is there a critical path to deliver Hybrid Sharepoint results?

<--- Score

4. Is there any requirement of inbound/outbound fax?
<--- Score

5. Who are the Hybrid Sharepoint improvement team members, including Management Leads and Coaches?
<--- Score

6. What are the workloads regulatory and security requirements?
<--- Score

7. How do you keep key subject matter experts in the loop?
<--- Score

8. Are there any seasonal workforce requirements?
<--- Score

9. What critical content must be communicated – who, what, when, where, and how?
<--- Score

10. In the case that the hardware specified is not providing the desired throughput or failover capabilities, who is responsible for providing the additional equipment?
<--- Score

11. Is Hybrid Sharepoint linked to key stakeholder goals and objectives?
<--- Score

12. If substitutes have been appointed, have they been briefed on the Hybrid Sharepoint goals and received regular communications as to the progress to date?
<--- Score

13. How is the team tracking and documenting its work?
<--- Score

14. What are the compelling stakeholder reasons for embarking on Hybrid Sharepoint?
<--- Score

15. What are your office suite format requirements?
<--- Score

16. Is a unified view of external content required?
<--- Score

17. How will the Hybrid Sharepoint team and the group measure complete success of Hybrid Sharepoint?
<--- Score

18. Is the improvement team aware of the different versions of a process: what they think it is vs. what it actually is vs. what it should be vs. what it could be?
<--- Score

19. Will team members regularly document their Hybrid Sharepoint work?
<--- Score

20. How can a hybrid cloud strategy contribute to

the requirements for IT resilience?
<--- Score

21. How will variation in the actual durations of each activity be dealt with to ensure that the expected Hybrid Sharepoint results are met?
<--- Score

22. Is there a Hybrid Sharepoint management charter, including stakeholder case, problem and goal statements, scope, milestones, roles and responsibilities, communication plan?
<--- Score

23. When are meeting minutes sent out? Who is on the distribution list?
<--- Score

24. Will team members perform Hybrid Sharepoint work when assigned and in a timely fashion?
<--- Score

25. Hybrid clouds have unique security requirements that legacy security cannot meet. Since traditional security tools provide limited visibility into cloud infrastructure, how are you going to protect what you can not see?
<--- Score

26. Is there regularly 100% attendance at the team meetings? If not, have appointed substitutes attended to preserve cross-functionality and full representation?
<--- Score

27. Is full participation by members in regularly held

team meetings guaranteed?
<--- Score

28. What would be required to implement this model in your organization?
<--- Score

29. How did the Hybrid Sharepoint manager receive input to the development of a Hybrid Sharepoint improvement plan and the estimated completion dates/times of each activity?
<--- Score

30. What key stakeholder process output measure(s) does Hybrid Sharepoint leverage and how?
<--- Score

31. How often are the team meetings?
<--- Score

32. What customer feedback methods were used to solicit their input?
<--- Score

33. Has a high-level 'as is' process map been completed, verified and validated?
<--- Score

34. What constraints exist that might impact the team?
<--- Score

35. Have the customer needs been translated into specific, measurable requirements? How?
<--- Score

36. Is the team equipped with available and reliable resources?
<--- Score

37. How does the Hybrid Sharepoint manager ensure against scope creep?
<--- Score

38. How much elasticity do your workloads require?
<--- Score

39. Is there a completed, verified, and validated high-level 'as is' (not 'should be' or 'could be') stakeholder process map?
<--- Score

40. Are the regulatory requirements included in the scope of services?
<--- Score

41. When is/was the Hybrid Sharepoint start date?
<--- Score

42. Has everyone on the team, including the team leaders, been properly trained?
<--- Score

43. Has the direction changed at all during the course of Hybrid Sharepoint? If so, when did it change and why?
<--- Score

44. How was the 'as is' process map developed, reviewed, verified and validated?
<--- Score

45. Is the team formed and are team leaders (Coaches and Management Leads) assigned?
<--- Score

46. Are customer(s) identified and segmented according to their different needs and requirements?
<--- Score

47. What are the boundaries of the scope? What is in bounds and what is not? What is the start point? What is the stop point?
<--- Score

48. Is the team sponsored by a champion or stakeholder leader?
<--- Score

49. Are employee background checks required?
<--- Score

50. Has the Hybrid Sharepoint work been fairly and/or equitably divided and delegated among team members who are qualified and capable to perform the work? Has everyone contributed?
<--- Score

51. Does the team have regular meetings?
<--- Score

52. Has a team charter been developed and communicated?
<--- Score

53. Are customers identified and high impact areas defined?

<--- Score

54. Are team charters developed?
<--- Score

55. Is there a completed SIPOC representation, describing the Suppliers, Inputs, Process, Outputs, and Customers?
<--- Score

56. Do the problem and goal statements meet the SMART criteria (specific, measurable, attainable, relevant, and time-bound)?
<--- Score

57. What specifically is the problem? Where does it occur? When does it occur? What is its extent?
<--- Score

58. Does your organization have a clear business case for SharePoint. Why do you want it?
<--- Score

59. Will sharepoint be implemented on premise, hosted with a 3rd party provider, or in the cloud (sharepoint online). will a hybrid implementation be a requirement?
<--- Score

60. Has the improvement team collected the 'voice of the customer' (obtained feedback – qualitative and quantitative)?
<--- Score

61. Is the Hybrid Sharepoint scope manageable?
<--- Score

62. Are there any constraints known that bear on the ability to perform Hybrid Sharepoint work? How is the team addressing them?
<--- Score

63. What are the Roles and Responsibilities for each team member and its leadership? Where is this documented?
<--- Score

64. What are the dynamics of the communication plan?
<--- Score

65. Are improvement team members fully trained on Hybrid Sharepoint?
<--- Score

66. Is Hybrid Sharepoint currently on schedule according to the plan?
<--- Score

67. What are the rough order estimates on cost savings/opportunities that Hybrid Sharepoint brings?
<--- Score

68. Is the current 'as is' process being followed? If not, what are the discrepancies?
<--- Score

69. How do you define cloud computing?
<--- Score

70. What level of integration is required with SharePoint?

<--- Score

71. Are different versions of process maps needed to account for the different types of inputs?
<--- Score

72. Is a fully trained team formed, supported, and committed to work on the Hybrid Sharepoint improvements?
<--- Score

73. What would be the goal or target for a Hybrid Sharepoint's improvement team?
<--- Score

74. When is the estimated completion date?
<--- Score

75. Are stakeholder processes mapped?
<--- Score

76. What is a good case study for the use of Sharepoint as a tool for collaboration in an organization or network?
<--- Score

77. Are there different segments of customers?
<--- Score

78. Has a project plan, Gantt chart, or similar been developed/completed?
<--- Score

79. How are your hybrid cloud partners SLAs defined?
<--- Score

80. Has anyone else (internal or external to the group) attempted to solve this problem or a similar one before? If so, what knowledge can be leveraged from these previous efforts?
<--- Score

81. Is the team adequately staffed with the desired cross-functionality? If not, what additional resources are available to the team?
<--- Score

82. Which characteristics do you believe are hybrid cloud requirements?
<--- Score

Add up total points for this section:
_____ = Total points for this section

Divided by: _____ (number of statements answered) = _____
Average score for this section

Transfer your score to the Hybrid Sharepoint Index at the beginning of the Self-Assessment.

CRITERION #3: MEASURE:

INTENT: Gather the correct data. Measure the current performance and evolution of the situation.

In my belief, the answer to this question is clearly defined:

5 Strongly Agree

4 Agree

3 Neutral

2 Disagree

1 Strongly Disagree

1. What data was collected (past, present, future/ongoing)?
<--- Score

2. What is the impact of hybrid cloud computing on IT Operations?
<--- Score

3. Do you have an accurate cost analysis of cloud

usage in a hybrid cloud environment?
<--- Score

4. Is data collection planned and executed?
<--- Score

5. What tools are used for analysis /reporting?
<--- Score

6. Are there cost for back up clouds?
<--- Score

7. Is key measure data collection planned and executed, process variation displayed and communicated and performance baselined?
<--- Score

8. Was a data collection plan established?
<--- Score

9. What has the team done to assure the stability and accuracy of the measurement process?
<--- Score

10. What is the total solution cost?
<--- Score

11. What cloud alternative (Private, Hybrid, Public, etc.) is the target of analysis?
<--- Score

12. What does the cloud cost?
<--- Score

13. Is data collected on key measures that were identified?

<--- Score

14. Is Hybrid Cloud worth the cost and effort?
<--- Score

15. What is the impact of hybrid cloud computing on i&o?
<--- Score

16. Given the popularity of hybrid and multi-cloud deployment models, how do you drive the right operational and cost visibility insights for your workloads?
<--- Score

17. How large is the gap between current performance and the customer-specified (goal) performance?
<--- Score

18. How much does the disaster recovery process cost?
<--- Score

19. Have you found any 'ground fruit' or 'low-hanging fruit' for immediate remedies to the gap in performance?
<--- Score

20. What does it cost to run your current infrastructure?
<--- Score

21. What system changes would cause the integrity check on your operating system drive to fail?

<--- Score

22. How do you measure the cost of your private cloud?

<--- Score

23. Is a solid data collection plan established that includes measurement systems analysis?
<--- Score

24. What will it cost to run your infrastructure on a cloud platform?

<--- Score

25. What particular quality tools did the team find helpful in establishing measurements?
<--- Score

26. What are the key input variables? What are the key process variables? What are the key output variables?
<--- Score

27. How can you measure Hybrid Cloud health?

<--- Score

28. What is the true cost of running your private cloud?

<--- Score

29. Who participated in the data collection for measurements?
<--- Score

30. What disruptions will Hybrid Cloud cause?

<--- Score

31. How do you track cloud cost changes?
<--- Score

32. How do you propose to provide and measure performance?
<--- Score

33. Are process variation components displayed/communicated using suitable charts, graphs, plots?
<--- Score

34. How is workload and performance measured?
<--- Score

35. What does this location cost in terms of operating expenses?
<--- Score

36. Are you ready to focus on the total customer experience?
<--- Score

37. Has the impact of cost overruns been analyzed?
<--- Score

38. What is the most cost-effective way to reduce the risk?
<--- Score

39. Is Process Variation Displayed/Communicated?
<--- Score

40. Are high impact defects defined and identified in the stakeholder process?
<--- Score

41. Do you have a roadmap for enterprise analytics?

<--- Score

42. What key measures identified indicate the performance of the stakeholder process?
<--- Score

43. Has the impact of late delivery been analyzed?
<--- Score

44. What does this location cost in terms of capital and operating expenses?
<--- Score

45. Are key measures identified and agreed upon?
<--- Score

46. With so much focus on the cloud today, what are the pros and cons of cloud, Hybrid, On-Premise, and other delivery models for your organizations ERP solution?
<--- Score

47. What charts has the team used to display the components of variation in the process?
<--- Score

48. Are documents impacted by the GRC solution stored exclusively in SharePoint?
<--- Score

49. What are the agreed upon definitions of the high impact areas, defect(s), unit(s), and opportunities that will figure into the process capability metrics?

<--- Score

50. Is long term and short term variability accounted for?
<--- Score

51. Is there a Performance Baseline?
<--- Score

Add up total points for this section:
_____ = Total points for this section

Divided by: _____ (number of statements answered) = _____
Average score for this section

Transfer your score to the Hybrid Sharepoint Index at the beginning of the Self-Assessment.

CRITERION #4: ANALYZE:

INTENT: Analyze causes, assumptions and hypotheses.

In my belief, the answer to this question is clearly defined:

5 Strongly Agree

4 Agree

3 Neutral

2 Disagree

1 Strongly Disagree

1. Do the shared drives you work with follow a common directory naming structure?
<--- Score

2. Where do applications and data need to be located?
<--- Score

3. How do you capture and harness the data?
<--- Score

4. What were the financial benefits resulting from any 'ground fruit or low-hanging fruit' (quick fixes)?
<--- Score

5. What data and data types do you need?
<--- Score

6. Will they help you restore your data when it is corrupt or lost?
<--- Score

7. Who has ownership of data in a cloud model?
<--- Score

8. How do you improve business processes and how do you deliver on that?
<--- Score

9. Can they tell where your data physically resides?
<--- Score

10. What are the drivers for this rapid adoption and disruption in the traditional IT world?
<--- Score

11. Does your organization need to protect data at rest?
<--- Score

12. Where should your backup or archive data be stored?
<--- Score

13. Can you move your data and application from one provider to another?

<--- Score

14. How is the data handled?
<--- Score

15. Regarding the existing data what is the format?
<--- Score

16. What are the business drivers?
<--- Score

17. Can data be encrypted in the cloud environment?
<--- Score

18. How to get data out?
<--- Score

19. Who has access to the data?
<--- Score

20. Why put applications and data in the cloud?
<--- Score

21. Does your data storage work as hard as it should?
<--- Score

22. Where is the data stored?
<--- Score

23. What areas of your organization need a baseline level of data protection?
<--- Score

24. How does your organization decide where to put data on a hybrid cloud and how to use it?
<--- Score

25. How fast does it take to recover data from your cloud?
<--- Score

26. How will your existing technology stack, designed to support your ERP system, interface with the new data coming from the cloud?
<--- Score

27. How much data will you share?
<--- Score

28. How long will you retain data in the storage cloud?
<--- Score

29. Who would have drafted the data sharing agreements to be reviewed?
<--- Score

30. Does your application show user permissions for files in Microsoft OneDrive?
<--- Score

31. Where is your data stored?
<--- Score

32. Do you use end-to-end hybrid cloud data solutions?
<--- Score

33. Technology drivers: what were the primary

technical challenges your organization faced?

<--- Score

34. Is your data storage solution up to the job?

<--- Score

35. Does the cloud service provider support the necessary management processes?

<--- Score

36. What happens to the data if the provider goes under?

<--- Score

37. Is your data lost if the data center is lost?

<--- Score

38. Who drives tech adoption and why?

<--- Score

39. How can data exfiltration be detected and stopped?

<--- Score

40. Business Drivers: Describe the primary business drivers for your initiative. What business challenges were faced?

<--- Score

41. Who has ownership of data in the cloud model?

<--- Score

42. Who protects your cloud data?

<--- Score

43. What is the data-backup process?

<--- Score

44. Does your kubernetes solution equally support the private data center and public cloud endpoints that your business needs to deliver kubernetes on?
<--- Score

45. How critical is your business data?
<--- Score

46. How does the provider protect data?
<--- Score

47. What is the data-recovery process?
<--- Score

48. How can data be protected in the process of transferring and storing it in the cloud?
<--- Score

49. How can data interoperability be accommodated?
<--- Score

50. Is your data safe when it is on one public cloud?
<--- Score

51. How is your data being protected?
<--- Score

52. What is the applicable data model?
<--- Score

53. What data and services will it depend on?

<--- Score

54. Are your data models consistent?
<--- Score

55. How will you do content management to refresh data?
<--- Score

56. How will data be protected, conveyed, and destroyed?
<--- Score

57. Can you use cloud-based data to train machine learning models?
<--- Score

58. What is the sensitivity of the data in the system or the system functionality?
<--- Score

59. Is there any script to upload data?
<--- Score

60. What tools are best for processing fragmented data?
<--- Score

61. Do your applications include DLP (Data Loss Protection) capabilities?
<--- Score

62. What percentage of your organizations data is in the cloud?
<--- Score

63. Who has access to customer data?
<--- Score

64. What is the lineage of your data and its life cycle transformation?
<--- Score

65. Does your application show data business owners?
<--- Score

66. What is the best approach for working with data in a hybrid cloud?
<--- Score

67. How to move large amounts of data to public cloud?
<--- Score

68. What is the disaster-recovery process?
<--- Score

69. How exposed is your data to being lost?
<--- Score

70. In what format will the data be provided for transition?
<--- Score

71. If you go out of business, how will your organization gain access to the data?
<--- Score

72. Data location: does the provider allow for any control over the location of data?
<--- Score

73. High availability and disaster recovery do you need high availability and disaster recovery for this application/data in the cloud?

<--- Score

74. What is the data jurisdiction?

<--- Score

75. What tools were used to narrow the list of possible causes?

<--- Score

76. Do you need to retain the data for any reason?

<--- Score

77. What ERP data can be kept on premise and what can be moved to the cloud?

<--- Score

78. What is the Data availability management and disaster recovery?

<--- Score

79. Where does your data already live?

<--- Score

80. How much data growth do you expect this year?

<--- Score

81. Is your data heavily regulated?

<--- Score

82. Where do the application and data need to be located?

<--- Score

83. How do you know your data is secure?
<--- Score

84. For what application is the data used?
<--- Score

85. Is your data up to date and accurate?
<--- Score

86. How do you classify data for private/public cloud?
<--- Score

87. How often is the data backed up?
<--- Score

88. How much do you know about your data backup process?
<--- Score

89. What is the disaster recovery process?
<--- Score

90. Does data in motion and at rest need to be encrypted?
<--- Score

91. What were the crucial 'moments of truth' on the process map?
<--- Score

92. What level of data protection and disaster recovery does it require?
<--- Score

93. What are the data retention requirements?
<--- Score

94. Is the contractor responsible for implementing a backup strategy to minimize loss of data?
<--- Score

95. Are you comfortable housing your data in the cloud?
<--- Score

96. Do you really need all that data on disk?
<--- Score

97. How can you avoid data chaos?
<--- Score

98. Do you have a mission critical database environment?
<--- Score

99. Is data center and infrastructure engineering a critical differentiator?
<--- Score

100. Data governance and security: how do you secure the data across all environments and which access control needs to be in place?
<--- Score

101. Is there a file size limit for searching data?
<--- Score

102. Do you require full control over all data and systems?

<--- Score

103. Can you ensure chain of custody for sensitive data?

<--- Score

104. Can important data be entrusted to the cloud?

<--- Score

105. What is the difference between Enterprise Information Management and Data Warehousing?

<--- Score

106. Where are the locations for uploading data?

<--- Score

107. Does the hosted provider utilize a public or hybrid cloud, which may expose customer data to the possibility of being captured?

<--- Score

108. Does your application search files in cloud storage Microsoft OneDrive?

<--- Score

109. In which jurisdiction or country will data be stored?

<--- Score

110. What is a breach of data?

<--- Score

111. Is the data stored in a private or a public cloud?

<--- Score

112. Where are your users putting data?
<--- Score

113. What are the main drivers in moving to the cloud?
<--- Score

114. How is your data secured?
<--- Score

115. How easy it to access your data?
<--- Score

116. What are the target business processes your organization would like to improve with this initial project?
<--- Score

117. How are on-premises security processes and solutions adapted in hybrid cloud?
<--- Score

118. Where should your users BYOD data be stored?
<--- Score

119. What devices have access to your data in the cloud?
<--- Score

120. Where are internal and cloud datasets combined?
<--- Score

121. Word processing applications: one or several?

<--- Score

122. Can you protect all of your organizations data?
<--- Score

123. Do data in motion and at rest need to be encrypted?
<--- Score

124. Whats the process to create a site?
<--- Score

125. Just how secure is your data?
<--- Score

126. What is the default data set or software package that a client is entitled to?
<--- Score

127. Security is an issue, does the hosted provider utilize a public or hybrid cloud, which may expose customer data to the possibility of being captured?
<--- Score

128. Who is responsible to look after data over the cloud?
<--- Score

129. Can you trust your data?
<--- Score

130. What Hybrid Cloud is used for processing?
<--- Score

Add up total points for this section:
_____ = Total points for this section

Divided by: _____ (number of statements answered) = _____
Average score for this section

Transfer your score to the Hybrid Sharepoint Index at the beginning of the Self-Assessment.

CRITERION #5: IMPROVE:

INTENT: Develop a practical solution. Innovate, establish and test the solution and to measure the results.

In my belief, the answer to this question is clearly defined:

5 Strongly Agree

4 Agree

3 Neutral

2 Disagree

1 Strongly Disagree

1. Is a solution implementation plan established, including schedule/work breakdown structure, resources, risk management plan, cost/budget, and control plan?
<--- Score

2. What is your organizations roadmap for its products?
<--- Score

3. How important is time-to-market for added functionality or new solutions?

<--- Score

4. Is pilot data collected and analyzed?
<--- Score

5. How are your solutions different?

<--- Score

6. Is a contingency plan established?
<--- Score

7. How was your Hybrid Cloud strategy developed?

<--- Score

8. Can it integrate with your management solutions?

<--- Score

9. What are the potential risks, and how can they be mitigated?

<--- Score

10. What communications are necessary to support the implementation of the solution?
<--- Score

11. What is the implementation plan?
<--- Score

12. What lessons, if any, from a pilot were incorporated into the design of the full-scale solution?
<--- Score

13. How did the team generate the list of possible solutions?
<--- Score

14. **What SharePoint skills do you currently have in house in terms of SharePoint Administration, Maintenance, Content Owner/Authorship, and Development?**
<--- Score

15. **Is public, private or hybrid solution suitable for your applications?**
<--- Score

16. **Does your organization use Microsoft SharePoint Server (MOSS) for IT collaboration needs around the EDM solution?**
<--- Score

17. How will the group know that the solution worked?
<--- Score

18. Are improved process ('should be') maps modified based on pilot data and analysis?
<--- Score

19. What does the 'should be' process map/design look like?
<--- Score

20. **Which cloud services are solution candidates?**
<--- Score

21. What tools were used to tap into the creativity and encourage 'outside the box' thinking?

<--- Score

22. Why even consider Hybrid Cloud solutions?
<--- Score

23. Is your organization using hybrid cloud solutions?
<--- Score

24. What happens to the formatting of Word or other Office documents saved on Google Apps?
<--- Score

25. Are possible solutions generated and tested?
<--- Score

26. When thinking about risks related to using cloud services, what are your top concerns?
<--- Score

27. Can your system generate an electronic bill after the completion of a documented event?
<--- Score

28. What is happening with IT Operations and development?
<--- Score

29. Is there a cost/benefit analysis of optimal solution(s)?
<--- Score

30. What decisions do you need to make about the OU certifier to use for your mail servers?
<--- Score

31. How will the team or the process owner(s) monitor the implementation plan to see that it is working as intended?
<--- Score

32. Are the best solutions selected?
<--- Score

33. Does your organization intend to use Microsoft SharePoint web content management and publishing features outside of the EDM solution?
<--- Score

34. Was a pilot designed for the proposed solution(s)?
<--- Score

35. What will be the technology solutions for a hybrid private/public cloud use?
<--- Score

36. Which capabilities do you believe are most important to a systems management solution?
<--- Score

37. Were any criteria developed to assist the team in testing and evaluating potential solutions?
<--- Score

38. What tools were used to evaluate the potential solutions?
<--- Score

39. What attendant changes will need to be made to ensure that the solution is successful?
<--- Score

40. What are the risks of moving to cloud-based ERP and how do you manage them?
<--- Score

41. Is there a small-scale pilot for proposed improvement(s)? What conclusions were drawn from the outcomes of a pilot?
<--- Score

42. What is in your organizations risk registry?
<--- Score

43. Are there any requirements around storage design for your virtualized SharePoint solution?
<--- Score

44. What is the optimal cloud deployment model?
<--- Score

45. What were the underlying assumptions on the cost-benefit analysis?
<--- Score

46. Are new and improved process ('should be') maps developed?
<--- Score

47. What is the best way for you to engage with your technology provider to ensure you keep your environment optimized and stay aware of the next big thing?
<--- Score

48. Is the implementation plan designed?
<--- Score

49. What new capabilities need to be developed?
<--- Score

50. Is your organization looking for Microsoft SharePoint to be a read only consumption model, or a creation model for documents as well?
<--- Score

51. Are there any constraints (technical, political, cultural, or otherwise) that would inhibit certain solutions?
<--- Score

52. What error proofing will be done to address some of the discrepancies observed in the 'as is' process?
<--- Score

53. Who makes decisions about funding distribution (short-term and ongoing)?
<--- Score

54. What are the technology solutions for a hybrid private/public cloud use?
<--- Score

55. How does the solution remove the key sources of issues discovered in the analyze phase?
<--- Score

56. What are the risks associated in implementing cloud ERP?
<--- Score

57. How are you involved with network management products and solutions within your organization?

<--- Score

58. What network solutions will facilitate the implementation of a hybrid cloud?

<--- Score

59. How much risk are you comfortable with?

<--- Score

60. What is Hybrid Sharepoint's impact on utilizing the best solution(s)?

<--- Score

61. Is the optimal solution selected based on testing and analysis?

<--- Score

62. Can you have a hybrid solution for indirect spend?

<--- Score

63. To what extent have you tested and evaluated them?

<--- Score

64. How do hybrid backup solutions work?

<--- Score

65. Describe the design of the pilot and what tests were conducted, if any?

<--- Score

66. What is the optimal implementation strategy?

<--- Score

67. How do you develop a public cloud strategy?

<--- Score

68. What are the advantages of moving to a cloud solution?
<--- Score

69. Is software-defined networking (SDN) a solution to hybrid cloud networks?
<--- Score

70. Should you evaluate a hybrid cloud strategy?
<--- Score

71. What tools were most useful during the improve phase?
<--- Score

72. How do you evaluate solutions?
<--- Score

73. After your roadmap is laid out, what is next?
<--- Score

74. What is the team's contingency plan for potential problems occurring in implementation?
<--- Score

75. When should your organization evaluate its hybrid cloud strategy?
<--- Score

76. Are you developing a cloud portfolio?
<--- Score

77. How should security risks and challenges be addressed?

<--- Score

Add up total points for this section:
_____ = Total points for this section

Divided by: _____ (number of statements answered) = _____
Average score for this section

Transfer your score to the Hybrid Sharepoint Index at the beginning of the Self-Assessment.

CRITERION #6: CONTROL:

INTENT: Implement the practical solution. Maintain the performance and correct possible complications.

In my belief, the answer to this question is clearly defined:

5 Strongly Agree

4 Agree

3 Neutral

2 Disagree

1 Strongly Disagree

1. What are the tools the network operations team uses for network monitoring and troubleshooting?
<--- Score

2. How easy is it to scale up or down?
<--- Score

3. Does a troubleshooting guide exist or is it needed?
<--- Score

4. Is there a transfer of ownership and knowledge to process owner and process team tasked with the responsibilities.
<--- Score

5. Backup needs are often overlooked with hybrid clouds. Do you plan to use your legacy system to back up cloud-based virtual machines?
<--- Score

6. How will report readings be checked to effectively monitor performance?
<--- Score

7. Is a response plan established and deployed?
<--- Score

8. How do you monitor that you have enough capacity?
<--- Score

9. How do you go about building a suitable business plan for hybrid cloud?
<--- Score

10. What does it mean to scale?
<--- Score

11. Are there documented procedures?
<--- Score

12. Is knowledge gained on process shared and institutionalized?
<--- Score

13. What open standards does your cloud provider use?
<--- Score

14. Have new or revised work instructions resulted?
<--- Score

15. Are operating procedures consistent?
<--- Score

16. How will new or emerging customer needs/requirements be checked/communicated to orient the process toward meeting the new specifications and continually reducing variation?
<--- Score

17. How will the process owner and team be able to hold the gains?
<--- Score

18. Will any special training be provided for results interpretation?
<--- Score

19. What is your cloud data management plan?
<--- Score

20. Is there a documented and implemented monitoring plan?
<--- Score

21. As part of a governance plan, did you determine who does what? For example, who creates sites, who controls keywords in Search, or who manages the metadata and ensures that the metadata is applied correctly?

<--- Score

22. Do you have a plan for managing your sprawl?
<--- Score

23. How might the group capture best practices and lessons learned so as to leverage improvements?
<--- Score

24. Has the improved process and its steps been standardized?
<--- Score

25. What other systems, operations, processes, and infrastructures (hiring practices, staffing, training, incentives/rewards, metrics/dashboards/scorecards, etc.) need updates, additions, changes, or deletions in order to facilitate knowledge transfer and improvements?
<--- Score

26. What are the plans to utilize SDN?
<--- Score

27. What is the control/monitoring plan?
<--- Score

28. What are your Hybrid Cloud options to scale?
<--- Score

29. Will it become your corporate standard for user file sharing?
<--- Score

30. Does job training on the documented procedures need to be part of the process team's education and

training?
<--- Score

31. What are your future cloud storage plans?
<--- Score

32. How is security monitored across hybrid cloud services?
<--- Score

33. Does the Hybrid Sharepoint performance meet the customer's requirements?
<--- Score

34. Is there a recommended audit plan for routine surveillance inspections of Hybrid Sharepoint's gains?
<--- Score

35. Do data and technology standards have to be developed?
<--- Score

36. Are new process steps, standards, and documentation ingrained into normal operations?
<--- Score

37. What quality tools were useful in the control phase?
<--- Score

38. How do you plan to deploy the clients?
<--- Score

39. What are the critical parameters to watch?
<--- Score

40. Are documented procedures clear and easy to follow for the operators?
<--- Score

41. How will the process owner verify improvement in present and future sigma levels, process capabilities?
<--- Score

42. Is there a control plan in place for sustaining improvements (short and long-term)?
<--- Score

43. Is there a standardized process?
<--- Score

44. How can you better control, manage, and secure corresponding environments and your workloads?
<--- Score

45. How do you monitor usage across clouds ?
<--- Score

46. What should the next improvement project be that is related to Hybrid Sharepoint?
<--- Score

47. Is reporting being used or needed?
<--- Score

48. Is the document/deliverable developed per the appropriate or required standards (for example, Institute of Electrical and Electronics Engineers standards)?
<--- Score

49. How will the day-to-day responsibilities for monitoring and continual improvement be transferred from the improvement team to the process owner?
<--- Score

50. Is new knowledge gained imbedded in the response plan?
<--- Score

51. How can you monitor and support the solution if it fails?
<--- Score

52. What other areas of the group might benefit from the Hybrid Sharepoint team's improvements, knowledge, and learning?
<--- Score

53. Do you actively monitor performance of your cloud-based applications?
<--- Score

54. Are suggested corrective/restorative actions indicated on the response plan for known causes to problems that might surface?
<--- Score

55. Does the application scale vertically or horizontally?
<--- Score

56. How will your IT infrastructure scale and evolve over the next three to five years?
<--- Score

57. Is there documentation that will support the successful operation of the improvement?
<--- Score

58. What key inputs and outputs are being measured on an ongoing basis?
<--- Score

59. How will input, process, and output variables be checked to detect for sub-optimal conditions?
<--- Score

60. Is the plan to use SharePoint for collaboration (WIP) content and controlled records?
<--- Score

61. Is the data backup plan sufficient to meet your organizations need?
<--- Score

62. Is a response plan in place for when the input, process, or output measures indicate an 'out-of-control' condition?
<--- Score

63. What is the recommended frequency of auditing?
<--- Score

64. How do you scale data storages?
<--- Score

65. How important are standards for public storage clouds?
<--- Score

66. Does the response plan contain a definite closed

loop continual improvement scheme (e.g., plan-do-check-act)?
<--- Score

67. How do you scale up applications?
<--- Score

68. How does the application fit with technical standards?
<--- Score

69. Who is the Hybrid Sharepoint process owner?
<--- Score

70. What are your organizations plans for cloud computing?
<--- Score

Add up total points for this section:
_____ = Total points for this section

Divided by: _____ (number of statements answered) = _____
Average score for this section

Transfer your score to the Hybrid Sharepoint Index at the beginning of the Self-Assessment.

CRITERION #7: SUSTAIN:

INTENT: Retain the benefits.

In my belief, the answer to this question is clearly defined:

5 Strongly Agree

4 Agree

3 Neutral

2 Disagree

1 Strongly Disagree

1. How are the workloads backups currently performed?
<--- Score

2. How would you rate how well IT staff work together between IT departments?
<--- Score

3. Which public clouds and CSPs is your business using?
<--- Score

4. Why is Hybrid Cloud important?
<--- Score

5. What are the criteria your organization uses to select a cloud based system?
<--- Score

6. What is your projected date of implementation?
<--- Score

7. Can you obtain private cloud from any it vendor?
<--- Score

8. How can you support new container environments?
<--- Score

9. How do you select hybrid cloud storage architectures?
<--- Score

10. Is the user's business environment stable?
<--- Score

11. Will the public sector cloud deliver value?
<--- Score

12. How would this be deployed?
<--- Score

13. Are cloud providers oversubscribed?
<--- Score

14. Is the product easy to deploy?

<--- Score

15. What makes a cloud a cloud?
<--- Score

16. Can two internal approvals be reduced to one?
<--- Score

17. What happens if the power goes out?
<--- Score

18. How do you test the performance of the Cloud?
<--- Score

19. What about non production systems?
<--- Score

20. What is the pitch to Enterprise customers?
<--- Score

21. How do you get to the hybrid cloud?
<--- Score

22. How do you expect to be automating and orchestrating workloads on cloud platforms (PaaS) and/or infrastructure (IaaS) in 24 months?
<--- Score

23. Are you equipped to embark on this journey?
<--- Score

24. Where are the less obvious vulnerabilities in hybrid cloud environments?
<--- Score

25. What if the cloud goes down?

<--- Score

26. Will everything move to the cloud?
<--- Score

27. What are the current infrastructure capabilities?
<--- Score

28. When a user gets stuck, who do they call?
<--- Score

29. How sensitive to latency is your application?
<--- Score

30. What is the reputation of the public cloud provider?
<--- Score

31. Is it going to be on-premises, in the cloud, or a combination?
<--- Score

32. Which applications are best suited?
<--- Score

33. What are the business pain points?
<--- Score

34. How do you manage multiple clouds?
<--- Score

35. What do it managers expect from cloud computing?
<--- Score

36. What is cloud computing criticized for?
<--- Score

37. What is missing from the cloud?
<--- Score

38. What is the location of servers?
<--- Score

39. What are your storage clouds?
<--- Score

40. Is the application predictable and steady or volatile?
<--- Score

41. Do you have customers in regulated industries?
<--- Score

42. What does it mean to use hybrid?
<--- Score

43. What will your organization do with its savings?
<--- Score

44. How do you build a hybrid cloud that allows or supports elasticity?
<--- Score

45. How do you choose between cloud and onpremise?
<--- Score

46. Does any application have any insider threat

detection and response capability?
<--- Score

47. What is your implementation stage for cloud storage?
<--- Score

48. What is your strategy?
<--- Score

49. What benefits with a Hybrid Cloud will you have?
<--- Score

50. Do you want to allow requests to join/leave the group?
<--- Score

51. How far can you go with SharePoint for Enterprise Content Management?
<--- Score

52. What are users moving to the cloud for?
<--- Score

53. What cloud services are in use today?
<--- Score

54. If cutbacks in existing services are necessary, which services should be eliminated first?
<--- Score

55. What might you want to host in a public cloud?
<--- Score

56. Does it make sense to disrupt on-premises

workloads to transition to a hybrid cloud?
<--- Score

57. Does the application have Single Sign-On (SSO)?
<--- Score

58. Who uses this application?
<--- Score

59. What is between you and the cloud?
<--- Score

60. Is hybrid cloud the preferred enterprise model?
<--- Score

61. Why choose managed services?
<--- Score

62. What efforts have you invested in skilling your teams?
<--- Score

63. How long do you expect the application to live?
<--- Score

64. What does this change mean for the operations team?
<--- Score

65. Is the cloud service private, community, public, or hybrid?
<--- Score

**66. What should you expect from a self-service

cloud?

<--- Score

67. Who depends on this workload?

<--- Score

68. How do you build cloud native applications?

<--- Score

69. What makes a Hybrid Cloud team effective?

<--- Score

70. What is cloud computing to you?

<--- Score

71. What to do with inherited integration systems?

<--- Score

72. What is the exit strategy to leave O365?

<--- Score

73. What makes a strategy team effective?

<--- Score

74. How do you know that you are providing a cloud service, or when you are using a cloud service?

<--- Score

75. Is the cloud infrastructure performing as expected?

<--- Score

76. What can you implement as part of the project?

<--- Score

77. What forces are driving hybrid cloud adoption?

<--- Score

78. How is the cloud storage deployed?

<--- Score

79. How will the service provider respond to disasters and ensure continued service?

<--- Score

80. What if you approached the hybrid cloud differently?

<--- Score

81. What is the goal of a hybrid cloud system?

<--- Score

82. What are the differences between cloud ERP and on-premises ERP?

<--- Score

83. Is it stored in a compliant way?

<--- Score

84. What does the future hold?

<--- Score

85. When is the public cloud used as a test bed?

<--- Score

86. How can defenders perform effective incident response?

<--- Score

87. Whose cloud should you use?

<--- Score

88. Can you afford for technology to mature ?
<--- Score

89. How can or do licenses/subscriptions transfer?
<--- Score

90. What social Hybrid Cloud media platforms do you use?
<--- Score

91. Choosing your path to hybrid cloud: Buy or build?
<--- Score

92. At what stage of activity is your organization with respect to hybrid cloud infrastructure?
<--- Score

93. Should you choose managed services?
<--- Score

94. Is the cloud more secure?
<--- Score

95. Is Augmented Reality code allowed in sharepoint online?
<--- Score

96. How do you procure services for the cloud?
<--- Score

97. How long has the vendor been in business?
<--- Score

98. Which do you consider the most important

benefits of Hybrid Cloud (versus a non-hybrid cloud) environment?

<--- Score

99. Are you meeting the objectives of the client?

<--- Score

100. Why move toward hybrid cloud?

<--- Score

101. How well prepared is your organization for migrations?

<--- Score

102. Where can you see activities such as supplier enablement?

<--- Score

103. How likely is it that the service will work as expected?

<--- Score

104. Where is this Going?

<--- Score

105. Why is this so important in the cloud?

<--- Score

106. What are the downsides of the hybrid system?

<--- Score

107. Do you have a seamless and configurable network integration?

<--- Score

108. Where is your mail server?

<--- Score

109. What systems really matter?
<--- Score

110. What does it take to connect to the Cloud?
<--- Score

111. How do you minimize your use of sensitive PII?
<--- Score

112. How to overcome dependability?
<--- Score

113. What is the current number of deployed SharePoint users across the enterprise?
<--- Score

114. When is adopting a cloud-based ERP system the right choice?
<--- Score

115. Must you combine patterns of adoption?
<--- Score

116. Can you account for the design principles behind the clouds security?
<--- Score

117. Does everyone really want hybrid cloud?
<--- Score

118. What is future of Private cloud?
<--- Score

119. How many client access licenses (CALs) does the organization own for MOSS Enterprise?
<--- Score

120. What services are typically delivered?
<--- Score

121. How do you ensure your cloud is secure?
<--- Score

122. Which do you consider the most important challenges of Hybrid Cloud (versus a non-hybrid cloud environment)?
<--- Score

123. Where are the encryption keys stored?
<--- Score

124. How do you build a hybrid cloud?
<--- Score

125. Can you use this with SharePoint?
<--- Score

126. How does this relate to the questions of consolidation and fragmentation?
<--- Score

127. Can you bring your existing virtual machines and licensed applications into it?
<--- Score

128. Which cloud providers can host your applications?
<--- Score

129. Cloud, on-premise or hybrid?
<--- Score

130. What does hybrid mean to you?
<--- Score

131. What are you trying to accomplish?
<--- Score

132. How will you use the public cloud?
<--- Score

133. Who does which activities in the Migration flow?
<--- Score

134. What reverse proxies are supported?
<--- Score

135. Is recovery a blind spot for hybrid cloud backup?
<--- Score

136. How do you do Disaster Recovery ?
<--- Score

137. How is your cloud scalable?
<--- Score

138. What are your primary hybrid cloud goals?
<--- Score

139. Why hybrid cloud, why now?
<--- Score

140. How important is the workload to the

business?

<--- Score

141. Is cloud a good fit for this request?

<--- Score

142. What type of cloud service are you currently using?

<--- Score

143. What is the business criticality of the application?

<--- Score

144. Is your enterprise future-ready?

<--- Score

145. Does it matter where it lives?

<--- Score

146. Why do you use multiple cloud platforms?

<--- Score

147. Does the sharepoint portal use an existing single sign-on system like ldap or active directory?

<--- Score

148. Where do you run it?

<--- Score

149. What cloud services do you want to use?

<--- Score

150. What are the options for Service Provisioning?

<--- Score

151. When do you want installation?
<--- Score

152. How does your organization approach the SharePoint Deployment Conundrum: On-premises, Cloud or Hybrid?
<--- Score

153. Basic choice: shared tenant or separate tenants?
<--- Score

154. How can the Hybrid Cloud help?
<--- Score

155. How can you make it enterprise-class?
<--- Score

156. Are architect services provided?
<--- Score

157. How does advance access scheduling work?
<--- Score

158. What is not a cloud?
<--- Score

159. What do end users expect of Cloud Computing?
<--- Score

160. Will private cloud adoption increase?
<--- Score

161. Why switch from traditional it to the cloud?

<--- Score

162. How long does it really take to stand up a hybrid cloud?

<--- Score

163. Are they really as safe as they claim to be?

<--- Score

164. How do you manage security in your public cloud environment?

<--- Score

165. What hybrid cloud model is best?

<--- Score

166. Are there existing infrastructures that are serving as a barrier?

<--- Score

167. How do you use SaaS to secure multitier hybrid apps running on vsphere, vmware cloud on aws, and aws native?

<--- Score

168. Which authentication mechanism do you use?

<--- Score

169. How do you build and deploy cloud native apps?

<--- Score

170. What is the future for cloud based ERP?

<--- Score

**171. How well are vendors positioned to capture

this shift?
<--- Score

172. What services can integrate?
<--- Score

173. What areas in your business are suitable to move into the cloud now, or in the future?
<--- Score

174. Which cloud service model fits the business request?
<--- Score

175. Where does your Hybrid Cloud get updates?
<--- Score

176. Hybrid cloud - what kinds of capabilities?
<--- Score

177. Are you compliant with GDPR?
<--- Score

178. What are the cloud providers auditing procedures?
<--- Score

179. Can the application be containerized?
<--- Score

180. Have you ever had to replace or fire a cloud or SaaS provider?
<--- Score

181. What are you looking to track as vendor performance?

<--- Score

182. What do you want to accomplish?
<--- Score

183. What factors are driving the change?
<--- Score

184. Which vendors are your peers choosing?
<--- Score

185. Why is this important?
<--- Score

186. How can you center your security strategy around an NGFW if it does not integrate with the tools you are already invested in?
<--- Score

187. What are the vendor obligations?
<--- Score

188. What type of workloads are being placed on public cloud IaaS?
<--- Score

189. Will users be accessing applications in the cloud?
<--- Score

190. What core services should technology provide?
<--- Score

191. What is the relationship to other workloads?
<--- Score

192. How do you propose your organization request Key Management services?

<--- Score

193. Does the project support your core businesses?

<--- Score

194. Is the service Platform as a Service (PaaS)?

<--- Score

195. Why choose a hybrid cloud model?

<--- Score

196. How do you reduce application cycles?

<--- Score

197. Do you have the in-house personnel to fix what goes wrong?

<--- Score

198. Do the services innovate?

<--- Score

199. What are vendors asking?

<--- Score

200. How do you structure permissions in a site?

<--- Score

201. What else can you do in sharepoint?

<--- Score

202. Why did you pick what you picked as your first cloud application?

<--- Score

203. Are you ahead of your competitors or falling behind on cloud adoption?

<--- Score

204. Which hybrid topology should you use?

<--- Score

205. How many MOSS front ends does the organization currently have?

<--- Score

206. Which properties determine cloud adoption?

<--- Score

207. What does it mean to transform?

<--- Score

208. What is the security of the application?

<--- Score

209. Which network management functions are outsourced?

<--- Score

210. What makes an application portable?

<--- Score

211. What is driving hybrid cloud computing?

<--- Score

212. How do you ensure periodic reports on performance metrics?

<--- Score

213. What new opportunities will be provided and who will benefit?

<--- Score

214. Which approaches have you taken to cloud adoption?

<--- Score

215. Is your strategy built around Hybrid Cloud to last?

<--- Score

216. When to utilize SaaS applications?

<--- Score

217. From where do you get cloud storage?

<--- Score

218. Why deploy an enterprise hybrid cloud?

<--- Score

219. How do you ensure network multitenancy?

<--- Score

220. What kind of content will you have on it?

<--- Score

221. No doubt it is strategic to your business, and are you in the business of managing it?

<--- Score

222. Who has worked with this?

<--- Score

223. Is the cloud service SaaS, PaaS or IaaS?

<--- Score

224. Where can this workload go?
<--- Score

225. How can you ensure 100% uptime for cloud connections?
<--- Score

226. How do you Replace or Fire a Cloud Provider?
<--- Score

227. How do you choose the right direction and build the right strategy for your organization?
<--- Score

228. Is hybrid cloud actually possible?
<--- Score

229. What is a good user experience?
<--- Score

230. What type of change is coming?
<--- Score

231. What is your strategy going forward?
<--- Score

232. Can your application create specific accounts for people with no administrative rights (external auditors, non-IT executives, etc.), allowing them to perform audits securely and autonomously?
<--- Score

233. What is your Organizations level of cloud adoption?
<--- Score

234. What is the biggest security challenge for enterprise customers who are moving to hybrid cloud environments?
<--- Score

235. Cloud, on-premise, or hybrid?
<--- Score

236. How do you think the cloud system will affect your way of working?
<--- Score

237. How do you ensure application security?
<--- Score

238. How do your users access cloud services?
<--- Score

239. Single points of vulnerability?
<--- Score

240. What application server does it use?
<--- Score

241. Why the hybrid cloud?
<--- Score

242. What kind of cloud are you currently using?
<--- Score

243. How can you make it easy and innovation-ready?
<--- Score

244. Can you store everything in the cloud?

<--- Score

245. Why consider cloud hosting?
<--- Score

246. Is the cloud the right choice?
<--- Score

247. How do you integrate Hybrid Cloud into your environment?
<--- Score

248. Will the sharepoint portal use an existing single sign-on system like ldap or active directory?
<--- Score

249. When to go for a de-centralized hybrid testing model?
<--- Score

250. What applications are moving to cloud environments?
<--- Score

251. What are the patch management policies and procedures?
<--- Score

252. Can the applications be modified to run on the CSP supported OSs?
<--- Score

253. How quickly can the cloud service provider respond to questions?
<--- Score

254. How long will building the Hybrid Cloud take?
<--- Score

255. What are the main benefits of cloud ERP?
<--- Score

256. What is the maximum number of requests?
<--- Score

257. How important is this location to the business?
<--- Score

258. What types of cloud computing are in use (e.g., public, hybrid, and internal) and what are the legal and regulatory implications of use?
<--- Score

259. How can it infrastructure be offered dynamically over a network?
<--- Score

260. Are you using Microsoft SharePoint as an interface for Enterprise Applications?
<--- Score

261. How can it help?
<--- Score

262. What does hybrid cloud mean for your organization?
<--- Score

263. What is the hybrid cloud backup?
<--- Score

264. Where are your services running?

<--- Score

265. What cloud access and identity protocols are used?

<--- Score

266. What other services are available?

<--- Score

267. Does upper management support the project effort?

<--- Score

268. What makes a hybrid cloud service secure?

<--- Score

269. What resources (infrastructure and staff) do you have in the location?

<--- Score

270. What is the workload?

<--- Score

271. How well will the system work in the cloud?

<--- Score

272. Who are the Hybrid Cloud ERP vendors?

<--- Score

273. What does your cloud Team look like?

<--- Score

274. How do public and private clouds differ by functions?

<--- Score

275. Where does your DAM Strategy fit into Hybrid Cloud?

<--- Score

276. What is the Hybrid Cloud customer experience?

<--- Score

277. How is the workload protected?

<--- Score

278. What are the single sign on capabilities available?

<--- Score

279. What do customers have to say?

<--- Score

280. How will users sign-in to the cloud?

<--- Score

281. Will the business model work?

<--- Score

282. Does the hybrid cloud make sense for you?

<--- Score

283. What is your hybrid cloud strategy?

<--- Score

284. Are you providing the highest level of service?

<--- Score

285. When are you ready for it?

<--- Score

286. Are services effective in the Hybrid Cloud?
<--- Score

287. How do you connect your local private cloud to the external cloud?
<--- Score

288. What are the options of implementing business-aware hybrid cloud management tools?
<--- Score

289. What are you currently doing on premises and/or in the public cloud?
<--- Score

290. Level of indemnity provided by vendor or government?
<--- Score

291. How can you avoid creating a new cloud silo?
<--- Score

292. How much do you trust your cloud partner?
<--- Score

293. How will information be targeted at specific audiences?
<--- Score

294. What about portability of applications?
<--- Score

295. Does your application show user permissions for files in SharePoint Online?

<--- Score

296. Is the Hybrid Cloud team effective?
<--- Score

297. What slows down hybrid cloud adoption?
<--- Score

298. What does a hybrid cloud do for your business?
<--- Score

299. What are the advantages of a hybrid cloud?
<--- Score

300. Is your cloud infrastructure properly hardened and secured?
<--- Score

301. Is the cloud service provider financially stable?
<--- Score

302. How would you rate the communications between IT groups in other departments?
<--- Score

303. Which types of providers are being used by your organization?
<--- Score

304. Can your cloud use become too big to fail?
<--- Score

305. How do your network architectures affect cloud computing?

<--- Score

306. What does it mean to hybrid?
<--- Score

307. Which applications do you modernize?
<--- Score

308. What new applications and services are due to come online over the next year?
<--- Score

309. Is your total Hybrid Cloud rewards strategy in tune?
<--- Score

310. Should you be concerned about security?
<--- Score

311. Where should a workload go?
<--- Score

312. What are the collaboration tools available in SharePoint?
<--- Score

313. What service levels can you expect?
<--- Score

314. Is your enterprise ready for hybrid cloud?
<--- Score

315. Is this the way forward?
<--- Score

316. Why should you choose a private cloud?

<--- Score

317. How would you rate the IT efficiency in your department?
<--- Score

318. How do you target content to specific audiences?
<--- Score

319. Will you be able to tell which device the user conducted an activity on?
<--- Score

320. Why is your organization changing the way you work at this time?
<--- Score

321. How do you remove complexity from the implementation?
<--- Score

322. Is the primary CSC supporting an IT Operations role?
<--- Score

323. Does your organization use an intranet such as SharePoint as your information hub?
<--- Score

324. Are any existing applications monoliths?
<--- Score

325. What are the precise terms of 24/7 phone support?
<--- Score

326. What does higher protection enable?
<--- Score

327. What products and licenses are available?
<--- Score

328. What flavor of SharePoint do you use?
<--- Score

329. What does hybrid really mean?
<--- Score

330. Is there a formal Hybrid Cloud integration strategy?
<--- Score

331. How do you create your service-level agreements with cloud providers?
<--- Score

332. How will users access the applications?
<--- Score

333. What options does Google provide for offline access?
<--- Score

334. How do you consume a public cloud?
<--- Score

335. How protected are you as the business adopts Cloud and IoT?
<--- Score

336. What is the most compelling argument for

migrating your organizations technology to a cloud platform?
<--- Score

337. What information in the system is PII?
<--- Score

338. How do you address the already stated concerns?
<--- Score

339. Is a hybrid cloud affordable?
<--- Score

340. Will the vendor support a hybrid cloud environment?
<--- Score

341. What do you think is the future of the private cloud?
<--- Score

342. How can you create virtual network abstractions?
<--- Score

343. Are there benefits to your organization to pursue a single procurement for Microsoft licenses rather than separate purchases under separate EAs?
<--- Score

344. Why hybrid, why not all-in?
<--- Score

**345. How do you go about completing an

upgrade?

<--- Score

346. How the corporate Hybrid Cloud changed in the past year?

<--- Score

347. Cloud-native, on-premise or hybrid?

<--- Score

348. Are cloud team members committed fulltime?

<--- Score

349. Why cloud computing now ?

<--- Score

350. What can manage the complexity of hybrids?

<--- Score

351. Why does hybrid cloud make business sense?

<--- Score

352. Do you have dedicated IT staff to take care of back-end details and to configure, manage and support?

<--- Score

353. Will you protect your mission critical applications?

<--- Score

354. What do you want to Govern?

<--- Score

355. What are the security parameters in cloud computing?

<--- Score

356. Will users be accessing applications on-premises?
<--- Score

357. What if your workload runs in your private cloud?
<--- Score

358. How can you backup your applications?
<--- Score

359. Are you able to see a unified view of all the relevant metrics for your application?
<--- Score

360. Where are you thinking of putting it - the geographical location, the type of venue, the possible provider(s); and where are corresponding located in relation to the users?
<--- Score

361. Where does a hybrid cloud platform fit in?
<--- Score

362. How does multitenancy benefit the customer?
<--- Score

363. What are the benefits of hybrid cloud to your organization?
<--- Score

364. Why use a Hybrid approach?
<--- Score

365. How should you address social media and email requests for services?

<--- Score

366. What are the changes that come along with the cloud?

<--- Score

367. Where to get the skill set?

<--- Score

368. Which servers will function as your mail hub servers in the on-premises hub domain?

<--- Score

369. What challenges/barriers do you think there might be in the proposed system?

<--- Score

370. What is your role in dealing with ERP providers and customers who use ERP?

<--- Score

371. What can you not put in the Cloud?

<--- Score

372. Why edge computing and not simply cloud?

<--- Score

373. What types of hybrid are available?

<--- Score

374. What are your cloud rights?

<--- Score

375. Which cloud service is most appropriate for

your organization?
<--- Score

376. How do you set a default view for all of your e-mail folders?
<--- Score

377. What is holding back the cloud today?
<--- Score

378. Is your entire LAN connected to the cloud?
<--- Score

379. What applications could go to the cloud?
<--- Score

380. What are the main reasons for your organization to adopt cloud technology?
<--- Score

381. What do the customers want?
<--- Score

382. How do you feel about the public cloud?
<--- Score

383. Can you count on the provider to deliver the promised service?
<--- Score

384. Which languages will be installed and supported?
<--- Score

385. How do you move your organization towards Cloud?

<--- Score

386. How does licensing work in a SharePoint hybrid cloud?

<--- Score

387. How can cloud computing be leveraged appropriately?

<--- Score

388. What does your cloud architect do?

<--- Score

389. What does the adoption trend of cloud look like?

<--- Score

390. On-premise, cloud, or hybrid?

<--- Score

391. What services can be used in the cloud?

<--- Score

392. What is your organizations vision of cloud computing?

<--- Score

393. How is the hybrid cloud infrastructure built, integrated and managed?

<--- Score

394. What slows down public cloud adoption?

<--- Score

395. Is this a punishment or a reward?

<--- Score

396. Can you adopt a DevOps culture?
<--- Score

397. How do you protect your organizations content?
<--- Score

398. What are the technologies for cloud federation?
<--- Score

399. How exactly do you prioritize the migration of applications to the cloud?
<--- Score

400. Is the cloud service infrastructure available for use by any user?
<--- Score

401. Which service configuration do you use?
<--- Score

402. What is the lifecycle of a typical implementation?
<--- Score

403. Does support cover all the services that you use?
<--- Score

404. Is private or hybrid Cloud the best option for your organization?
<--- Score

405. Why should you choose hybrid cloud?

<--- Score

406. Do you want a public, private, or hybrid cloud?

<--- Score

407. Can you work across boundaries ?

<--- Score

408. What gives frontrunners competitive edge with hybrid?

<--- Score

409. What functionality is your organization looking to obtain from an e-mail archiving capability?

<--- Score

410. Where will your applications live?

<--- Score

411. What is the end result?

<--- Score

412. What are the business benefits of hybrid clouds?

<--- Score

413. How do you ensure appropriate security levels within your hybrid environment?

<--- Score

414. Which of your workloads are most suitable for cloud?

<--- Score

415. What is the Disaster Recovery service?
<--- Score

416. How are you choosing the best cloud adoption strategy for your business?
<--- Score

417. How is your Hybrid Cloud IoT enabled?
<--- Score

418. Can you safely manage delivery of the new breed of hybrid IT services?
<--- Score

419. What are the incident response guidelines?
<--- Score

420. Your business is cloud-ready, and is your network?
<--- Score

421. Who are the leaders in the cloud market?
<--- Score

422. How do you move workloads across your environments?
<--- Score

423. What are customers asking?
<--- Score

424. How do you manage workloads between clouds?
<--- Score

425. What do clients expect of the cloud?

<--- Score

426. What is the typical journey for a new customer?
<--- Score

427. Do you have the right partner in this journey?
<--- Score

428. Can you do complex searches with field qualifiers, bracketing/nesting of search terms along with Boolean operators such as AND, OR, NOT, NEAR?
<--- Score

429. How do you use powershell for performing operations in sharepoint?
<--- Score

430. Why is the workload running in this location?
<--- Score

431. Who manages this workload?
<--- Score

432. What storage or network should be used?
<--- Score

433. Who determines governance policies?
<--- Score

434. Will there be test groups, and who will be in them?
<--- Score

435. How are you automating and orchestrating

workloads on cloud platforms (PaaS) and/or infrastructure (IaaS) today?

<--- Score

436. What are your top concerns around hybrid cloud storage adoption?

<--- Score

437. Why use a hybrid cloud?

<--- Score

438. Are you running one application on one server?

<--- Score

439. What barriers do you think there might be for you in this proposed system?

<--- Score

440. What is your businesss strategy?

<--- Score

441. Do you currently use Modern SharePoint sites or pages?

<--- Score

442. Where do you find a cloud architect?

<--- Score

443. How do you manage a hybrid cloud environment?

<--- Score

444. Are your core systems premise or cloud, hybrid?

<--- Score

445. Where do you expect this to go?

<--- Score

446. How can you place workloads based on capacity, policy?

<--- Score

447. What is a realistic end state?

<--- Score

448. How do you know which cloud is best for you?

<--- Score

449. What are your Hybrid Cloud competency centers?

<--- Score

450. How do you become compliant?

<--- Score

451. What makes a cloud a hybrid cloud?

<--- Score

452. How safe is the cloud?

<--- Score

453. What type of cloud should you move to (private, hybrid, public)?

<--- Score

454. When should you consider a hybrid deployment?

<--- Score

**455. Which of your applications and services are

best suited for the cloud?

<--- Score

456. What is your Recovery point objective (rpo)?

<--- Score

457. How do you package and sell your support?

<--- Score

458. Which turnkey hybrid cloud model is right for your business?

<--- Score

459. How do you want to visualize your organization of your devices?

<--- Score

460. Are there better alternatives?

<--- Score

461. What leads to cloud ERP failures?

<--- Score

462. What are the infrastructure constraints?

<--- Score

463. Which applications profit from Cloud Computing?

<--- Score

464. Why hybrid cloud storage for backup and archive?

<--- Score

465. How do you ensure apps are portable between clouds?

<--- Score

466. Are some things just too cumbersome to do online?

<--- Score

467. Are you getting the full benefit?

<--- Score

468. What challenge does the hybrid cloud offer?

<--- Score

469. What steps do you think your organization should take to prepare for this change?

<--- Score

470. How do you propose integrating services?

<--- Score

471. What is driving the growth?

<--- Score

472. What existing Hybrid Cloud services exist?

<--- Score

473. How do topologies work in practice?

<--- Score

474. What is the cloud federation stack?

<--- Score

Add up total points for this section:
_____ = Total points for this section

Divided by: _____ (number of statements answered) = _____

Average score for this section

Transfer your score to the Hybrid Sharepoint Index at the beginning of the Self-Assessment.

Hybrid Sharepoint and Managing Projects, Criteria for Project Managers:

1.0 Initiating Process Group: Hybrid Sharepoint

1. What are the inputs required to produce the deliverables?

2. How well defined and documented were the Hybrid Sharepoint project management processes you chose to use?

3. Do you know the Hybrid Sharepoint projects goal, purpose and objectives?

4. What communication items need improvement?

5. Did the Hybrid Sharepoint project team have the right skills?

6. Establishment of pm office?

7. What will be the pressing issues of tomorrow?

8. Are the Hybrid Sharepoint project team and stakeholders meeting regularly and using a meeting agenda and taking notes to accurately document what is being covered and what happened in the weekly meetings?

9. Who is performing the work of the Hybrid Sharepoint project?

10. What are the overarching issues of your organization?

11. The Hybrid Sharepoint project you are managing

has nine stakeholders. How many channel of communications are there between corresponding stakeholders?

12. Which six sigma dmaic phase focuses on why and how defects and errors occur?

13. Measurable - are the targets measurable?

14. What input will you be required to provide the Hybrid Sharepoint project team?

15. What areas does the group agree are the biggest success on the Hybrid Sharepoint project?

16. What were things that you need to improve?

17. Just how important is your work to the overall success of the Hybrid Sharepoint project?

18. What is the NEXT thing to do?

19. How is each deliverable reviewed, verified, and validated?

20. How can you make your needs known?

1.1 Project Charter: Hybrid Sharepoint

21. For whom?

22. Who is the Hybrid Sharepoint project Manager?

23. Name and describe the elements that deal with providing the detail?

24. Did your Hybrid Sharepoint project ask for this?

25. What changes can you make to improve?

26. Why have you chosen the aim you have set forth?

27. What are the assigned resources?

28. Are you building in-house ?

29. Why is it important?

30. How will you learn more about the process or system you are trying to improve?

31. What material?

32. Who manages integration?

33. Pop quiz – which are the same inputs as in the Hybrid Sharepoint project charter?

34. Who will take notes, document decisions?

35. Customer: who are you doing the Hybrid Sharepoint project for?

36. Is time of the essence?

37. Hybrid Sharepoint project objective statement: what must the Hybrid Sharepoint project do?

38. What metrics could you look at?

39. What are the known stakeholder requirements?

40. What is the purpose of the Hybrid Sharepoint project?

1.2 Stakeholder Register: Hybrid Sharepoint

41. What is the power of the stakeholder?

42. How should employers make voices heard?

43. What & Why?

44. Who are the stakeholders?

45. What are the major Hybrid Sharepoint project milestones requiring communications or providing communications opportunities?

46. Is your organization ready for change?

47. Who is managing stakeholder engagement?

48. How much influence do they have on the Hybrid Sharepoint project?

49. How will reports be created?

50. Who wants to talk about Security?

51. How big is the gap?

52. What opportunities exist to provide communications?

1.3 Stakeholder Analysis Matrix: Hybrid Sharepoint

53. Identify the stakeholders levels most frequently used –or at least sought– in your Hybrid Sharepoint projects and for which purpose?

54. Economy - home, abroad?

55. Is there a reason why you are or are not not using an external rating system?

56. Do the stakeholders goals and expectations support or conflict with the Hybrid Sharepoint project goals?

57. Who will be affected by the work?

58. Beneficiaries; who are the potential beneficiaries?

59. Resources, assets, people?

60. Volumes, production, economies?

61. Who is influential in the Hybrid Sharepoint project area (both thematic and geographic areas)?

62. Supporters; who are the supporters?

63. Who can contribute financial or technical resources towards the work?

64. Will the impacts be local, national or international?

65. Political effects?

66. Technology development and innovation?

67. Cashflow, start-up cash-drain?

68. Which conditions out of the control of the management are crucial for the achievement of the immediate objective?

69. Opponents; who are the opponents?

70. Are there different rules or organizational models for men and women?

71. Are you going to weigh the stakeholders?

72. How affected by the problem(s)?

2.0 Planning Process Group: Hybrid Sharepoint

73. You are creating your WBS and find that you keep decomposing tasks into smaller and smaller units. How can you tell when you are done?

74. Is the identification of the problems, inequalities and gaps, with respective causes, clear in the Hybrid Sharepoint project?

75. How are the principles of aid effectiveness (ownership, alignment, management for development results and mutual responsibility) being applied in the Hybrid Sharepoint project?

76. What is the difference between the early schedule and late schedule?

77. How will users learn how to use the deliverables?

78. To what extent is the program helping to influence your organizations policy framework?

79. Mitigate. what will you do to minimize the impact should a risk event occur?

80. What makes your Hybrid Sharepoint project successful?

81. In what ways can the governance of the Hybrid Sharepoint project be improved so that it has greater likelihood of achieving future sustainability?

82. Will you be replaced?

83. What should you do next?

84. What is a Software Development Life Cycle (SDLC)?

85. If a task is partitionable, is this a sufficient condition to reduce the Hybrid Sharepoint project duration?

86. To what extent has a PMO contributed to raising the quality of the design of the Hybrid Sharepoint project?

87. Hybrid Sharepoint project assessment; why did you do this Hybrid Sharepoint project?

88. Who are the Hybrid Sharepoint project stakeholders?

89. Does it make any difference if you are successful?

90. Are there efficient coordination mechanisms to avoid overloading the counterparts, participating stakeholders?

91. If task x starts two days late, what is the effect on the Hybrid Sharepoint project end date?

2.1 Project Management Plan: Hybrid Sharepoint

92. Are the existing and future without-plan conditions reasonable and appropriate?

93. What worked well?

94. Who is the Hybrid Sharepoint project Manager?

95. Will you add a schedule and diagram?

96. Does the selected plan protect privacy?

97. What if, for example, the positive direction and vision of your organization causes expected trends to change resulting in greater need than expected?

98. Is there an incremental analysis/cost effectiveness analysis of proposed mitigation features based on an approved method and using an accepted model?

99. Is the budget realistic?

100. Who is the sponsor?

101. Are comparable cost estimates used for comparing, screening and selecting alternative plans, and has a reasonable cost estimate been developed for the recommended plan?

102. Is the appropriate plan selected based on your organizations objectives and evaluation criteria

expressed in Principles and Guidelines policies?

103. What is the business need?

104. What is Hybrid Sharepoint project scope management?

105. What would you do differently what did not work?

106. Are there any Client staffing expectations?

107. What are the constraints?

108. What should you drop in order to add something new?

109. What did not work so well?

2.2 Scope Management Plan: Hybrid Sharepoint

110. Does the Hybrid Sharepoint project have a Quality Culture?

111. Is the assigned Hybrid Sharepoint project manager a PMP (Certified Hybrid Sharepoint project manager) and experienced?

112. Does the title convey to the reader the essence of the Hybrid Sharepoint project?

113. What weaknesses do you have?

114. What strengths do you have?

115. Knowing the health of the Hybrid Sharepoint project – What is the status?

116. Are the results of quality assurance reviews provided to affected groups & individuals?

117. Is there a formal set of procedures supporting Issues Management?

118. Have all necessary approvals been obtained?

119. When will scope verification be performed?

120. Is quality monitored from the perspective of the customers needs and expectations?

121. Has a capability assessment been conducted?

122. Are software metrics formally captured, analyzed and used as a basis for other Hybrid Sharepoint project estimates?

123. Has stakeholder analysis been conducted, assessing influence on the Hybrid Sharepoint project and authority levels?

124. What is the most common tool for helping define the detail?

125. Is each item clearly and completely defined?

126. Are estimating assumptions and constraints captured?

127. Is there any form of automated support for Issues Management?

128. Cost / benefit analysis?

129. Are there any scope changes proposed for the previously authorized Hybrid Sharepoint project?

2.3 Requirements Management Plan: Hybrid Sharepoint

130. What are you trying to do?

131. Is there formal agreement on who has authority to approve a change in requirements?

132. Who came up with this requirement?

133. How knowledgeable is the primary Stakeholder(s) in the proposed application area?

134. How detailed should the Hybrid Sharepoint project get?

135. Will the contractors involved take full responsibility?

136. Did you provide clear and concise specifications?

137. Is the system software (non-operating system) new to the IT Hybrid Sharepoint project team?

138. Is the system software (non-operating system) new to the IT Hybrid Sharepoint project team?

139. Do you expect stakeholders to be cooperative?

140. Is any organizational data being used or stored?

141. How will you communicate scheduled tasks to other team members?

142. Will the product release be stable and mature enough to be deployed in the user community?

143. Will you perform a Requirements Risk assessment and develop a plan to deal with risks?

144. Will you document changes to requirements?

145. Is requirements work dependent on any other specific Hybrid Sharepoint project or non-Hybrid Sharepoint project activities (e.g. funding, approvals, procurement)?

146. What cost metrics will be used?

147. Could inaccurate or incomplete requirements in this Hybrid Sharepoint project create a serious risk for the business?

148. Has the requirements team been instructed in the Change Control process?

149. How will the information be distributed?

2.4 Requirements Documentation: Hybrid Sharepoint

150. Can the requirement be changed without a large impact on other requirements?

151. Who is interacting with the system?

152. How does what is being described meet the business need?

153. Does the system provide the functions which best support the customers needs?

154. Do technical resources exist?

155. What are the potential disadvantages/advantages?

156. What are current process problems?

157. Is the requirement realistically testable?

158. What is the risk associated with the technology?

159. How will they be documented / shared?

160. How much testing do you need to do to prove that your system is safe?

161. Who provides requirements?

162. Verifiability. can the requirements be checked?

163. Where do system and software requirements come from, what are sources?

164. Is the origin of the requirement clearly stated?

165. How much does requirements engineering cost?

166. What are the acceptance criteria?

167. Basic work/business process; high-level, what is being touched?

168. What is the risk associated with cost and schedule?

2.5 Requirements Traceability Matrix: Hybrid Sharepoint

169. How do you manage scope?

170. How small is small enough?

171. Why do you manage scope?

172. Do you have a clear understanding of all subcontracts in place?

173. What percentage of Hybrid Sharepoint projects are producing traceability matrices between requirements and other work products?

174. Is there a requirements traceability process in place?

175. What are the chronologies, contingencies, consequences, criteria?

176. How will it affect the stakeholders personally in career?

177. Describe the process for approving requirements so they can be added to the traceability matrix and Hybrid Sharepoint project work can be performed. Will the Hybrid Sharepoint project requirements become approved in writing?

178. What is the WBS?

179. Will you use a Requirements Traceability Matrix?

180. Why use a WBS?

2.6 Project Scope Statement: Hybrid Sharepoint

181. Change management vs. change leadership - what is the difference?

182. Are there adequate Hybrid Sharepoint project control systems?

183. Will the risk plan be updated on a regular and frequent basis?

184. What is change?

185. Has a method and process for requirement tracking been developed?

186. Is an issue management process documented and filed?

187. Risks?

188. Is the quality function identified and assigned?

189. Is there a Quality Assurance Plan documented and filed?

190. Is the plan for Hybrid Sharepoint project resources adequate?

191. Is the Hybrid Sharepoint project manager qualified and experienced in Hybrid Sharepoint project management?

192. Hybrid Sharepoint project lead, team lead, solution architect?

193. Are there backup strategies for key members of the Hybrid Sharepoint project?

194. Elements that deal with providing the detail?

195. Are there issues that could affect the existing requirements for the result, service, or product if the scope changes?

196. If there is an independent oversight contractor, have they signed off on the Hybrid Sharepoint project Plan?

197. Has the format for tracking and monitoring schedules and costs been defined?

2.7 Assumption and Constraint Log: Hybrid Sharepoint

198. Have all stakeholders been identified?

199. Is there documentation of system capability requirements, data requirements, environment requirements, security requirements, and computer and hardware requirements?

200. Has the approach and development strategy of the Hybrid Sharepoint project been defined, documented and accepted by the appropriate stakeholders?

201. Have adequate resources been provided by management to ensure Hybrid Sharepoint project success?

202. Has a Hybrid Sharepoint project Communications Plan been developed?

203. Does the document/deliverable meet all requirements (for example, statement of work) specific to this deliverable?

204. Are there unnecessary steps that are creating bottlenecks and/or causing people to wait?

205. Would known impacts serve as impediments?

206. Do the requirements meet the standards of correctness, completeness, consistency, accuracy, and

readability?

207. Are funding and staffing resource estimates sufficiently detailed and documented for use in planning and tracking the Hybrid Sharepoint project?

208. Is there adequate stakeholder participation for the vetting of requirements definition, changes and management?

209. Is the steering committee active in Hybrid Sharepoint project oversight?

210. Are formal code reviews conducted?

211. What to do at recovery?

212. Have the scope, objectives, costs, benefits and impacts been communicated to all involved and/or impacted stakeholders and work groups?

213. What is positive about the current process?

214. How can you prevent/fix violations?

215. What do you log?

2.8 Work Breakdown Structure: Hybrid Sharepoint

216. Is it still viable?

217. How much detail?

218. How many levels?

219. When would you develop a Work Breakdown Structure?

220. Why is it useful?

221. How big is a work-package?

222. Who has to do it?

223. When do you stop?

224. Why would you develop a Work Breakdown Structure?

225. What has to be done?

226. Is the work breakdown structure (wbs) defined and is the scope of the Hybrid Sharepoint project clear with assigned deliverable owners?

227. Can you make it?

228. What is the probability that the Hybrid Sharepoint project duration will exceed xx weeks?

229. When does it have to be done?

230. Where does it take place?

231. Is it a change in scope?

232. What is the probability of completing the Hybrid Sharepoint project in less that xx days?

2.9 WBS Dictionary: Hybrid Sharepoint

233. Budgets assigned to control accounts?

234. Is work properly classified as measured effort, LOE, or apportioned effort and appropriately separated?

235. Budgeted cost for work performed?

236. Is the work done on a work package level as described in the WBS dictionary?

237. Are management actions taken to reduce indirect costs when there are significant adverse variances?

238. Does the contractors system provide unit costs, equivalent unit or lot costs in terms of labor, material, other direct, and indirect costs?

239. Is subcontracted work defined and identified to the appropriate subcontractor within the proper WBS element?

240. Changes in the direct base to which overhead costs are allocated?

241. Does the contractors system include procedures for measuring performance of the lowest level organization responsible for the control account?

242. Are data being used by managers in an effective manner to ascertain Hybrid Sharepoint project or functional status, to identify reasons or significant variance, and to initiate appropriate corrective action?

243. Are budgets or values assigned to work packages and planning packages in terms of dollars, hours, or other measurable units?

244. Are all authorized tasks assigned to identified organizational elements?

245. Are overhead costs budgets established on a basis consistent with anticipated direct business base?

246. All cwbs elements specified for external reporting?

247. Are there procedures for monitoring action items and corrective actions to the point of resolution and are corresponding procedures being followed?

248. The already stated responsible for overhead performance control of related costs?

249. What are you counting on?

250. Identify and isolate causes of favorable and unfavorable cost and schedule variances?

251. Actual cost of work performed?

2.10 Schedule Management Plan: Hybrid Sharepoint

252. Were Hybrid Sharepoint project team members involved in the development of activity & task decomposition?

253. Has a Hybrid Sharepoint project Communications Plan been developed?

254. Is funded schedule margin reasonable and logically distributed?

255. Perform reality checks on schedules – are all tasks included?

256. Are the processes for schedule assessment and analysis defined?

257. After initial schedule development, will the schedule be reviewed and validated by the Hybrid Sharepoint project team?

258. Is there an approved case?

259. Is current scope of the Hybrid Sharepoint project substantially different than that originally defined?

260. Has a structured approach been used to break work effort into manageable components (WBS)?

261. Is Hybrid Sharepoint project status reviewed with the steering and executive teams at appropriate

intervals?

262. Have adequate resources been provided by management to ensure Hybrid Sharepoint project success?

263. Is the ims used by all levels of management for Hybrid Sharepoint project implementation and control?

264. Have external dependencies been captured in the schedule?

265. Is the schedule feasible and at what cost?

266. Are assumptions being identified, recorded, analyzed, qualified and closed?

267. Are right task and resource calendars used in the IMS?

268. Has the Hybrid Sharepoint project manager been identified?

269. Is a pmo (Hybrid Sharepoint project management office) in place and provide oversight to the Hybrid Sharepoint project?

270. Is the critical path valid?

2.11 Activity List: Hybrid Sharepoint

271. What did not go as well?

272. What are the critical bottleneck activities?

273. Should you include sub-activities?

274. How will it be performed?

275. What went wrong?

276. What is your organizations history in doing similar activities?

277. What will be performed?

278. How should ongoing costs be monitored to try to keep the Hybrid Sharepoint project within budget?

279. What is the probability the Hybrid Sharepoint project can be completed in xx weeks?

280. What went right?

281. The wbs is developed as part of a joint planning session. and how do you know that youhave done this right?

282. What is the LF and LS for each activity?

283. In what sequence?

284. When do the individual activities need to start

and finish?

285. How much slack is available in the Hybrid Sharepoint project?

286. Is infrastructure setup part of your Hybrid Sharepoint project?

287. For other activities, how much delay can be tolerated?

288. How can the Hybrid Sharepoint project be displayed graphically to better visualize the activities?

289. How do you determine the late start (LS) for each activity?

2.12 Activity Attributes: Hybrid Sharepoint

290. How many resources do you need to complete the work scope within a limit of X number of days?

291. How difficult will it be to do specific activities on this Hybrid Sharepoint project?

292. Activity: what is In the Bag?

293. Can more resources be added?

294. Where else does it apply?

295. Can you re-assign any activities to another resource to resolve an over-allocation?

296. Resource is assigned to?

297. Is there a trend during the year?

298. How much activity detail is required?

299. What is missing?

300. Activity: fair or not fair?

301. How many days do you need to complete the work scope with a limit of X number of resources?

302. Do you feel very comfortable with your prediction?

303. Are the required resources available or need to be acquired?

304. Have constraints been applied to the start and finish milestones for the phases?

305. Has management defined a definite timeframe for the turnaround or Hybrid Sharepoint project window?

306. Does your organization of the data change its meaning?

2.13 Milestone List: Hybrid Sharepoint

307. What are your competitors vulnerabilities?

308. What specific improvements did you make to the Hybrid Sharepoint project proposal since the previous time?

309. Sustainable financial backing?

310. What has been done so far?

311. Legislative effects?

312. How soon can the activity finish?

313. Gaps in capabilities?

314. Obstacles faced?

315. Loss of key staff?

316. What date will the task finish?

317. Effects on core activities, distraction?

318. What would happen if a delivery of material was one week late?

319. Do you foresee any technical risks or developmental challenges?

320. Milestone pages should display the UserID of the person who added the milestone. Does a report or query exist that provides this audit information?

321. Vital contracts and partners?

322. Timescales, deadlines and pressures?

323. How will you get the word out to customers?

324. Information and research?

2.14 Network Diagram: Hybrid Sharepoint

325. Where do you schedule uncertainty time?

326. What must be completed before an activity can be started?

327. What job or jobs could run concurrently?

328. Review the logical flow of the network diagram. Take a look at which activities you have first and then sequence the activities. Do they make sense?

329. If the Hybrid Sharepoint project network diagram cannot change and you have extra personnel resources, what is the BEST thing to do?

330. How confident can you be in your milestone dates and the delivery date?

331. Will crashing x weeks return more in benefits than it costs?

332. What job or jobs precede it?

333. What are the tools?

334. If x is long, what would be the completion time if you break x into two parallel parts of y weeks and z weeks?

335. What controls the start and finish of a job?

336. Exercise: what is the probability that the Hybrid Sharepoint project duration will exceed xx weeks?

337. What activities must follow this activity?

338. Planning: who, how long, what to do?

339. What job or jobs follow it?

340. Are the required resources available?

341. What is the lowest cost to complete this Hybrid Sharepoint project in xx weeks?

2.15 Activity Resource Requirements: Hybrid Sharepoint

342. What are constraints that you might find during the Human Resource Planning process?

343. Anything else?

344. Is there anything planned that does not need to be here?

345. When does monitoring begin?

346. Time for overtime?

347. Do you use tools like decomposition and rolling-wave planning to produce the activity list and other outputs?

348. What is the Work Plan Standard?

349. Which logical relationship does the PDM use most often?

350. Why do you do that?

351. Organizational Applicability?

352. How do you manage time?

353. How do you handle petty cash?

354. Are there unresolved issues that need to be

addressed?

355. Other support in specific areas?

356. How many signatures do you require on a check and does this match what is in your policy and procedures?

2.16 Resource Breakdown Structure: Hybrid Sharepoint

357. Why do you do it?

358. Goals for the Hybrid Sharepoint project. What is each stakeholders desired outcome for the Hybrid Sharepoint project?

359. What defines a successful Hybrid Sharepoint project?

360. Who will be used as a Hybrid Sharepoint project team member?

361. Who needs what information?

362. Changes based on input from stakeholders?

363. Who is allowed to perform which functions?

364. Who is allowed to see what data about which resources?

365. Why is this important?

366. What is each stakeholders desired outcome for the Hybrid Sharepoint project?

367. Which resources should be in the resource pool?

368. Is predictive resource analysis being done?

369. What are the requirements for resource data?

370. When do they need the information?

371. Why time management?

372. How should the information be delivered?

2.17 Activity Duration Estimates: Hybrid Sharepoint

373. Is a standard form used to obtain bids and proposals from prospective sellers?

374. If the optimiztic estimate for an activity is 12days, and the pessimistic estimate is 18days, what is the standard deviation of this activity?

375. What do corresponding sources say about Hybrid Sharepoint project management?

376. Which is a benefit of an analogous Hybrid Sharepoint project estimate?

377. Are procedures defined by which the Hybrid Sharepoint project scope may be changed?

378. Are activity dependencies identified?

379. Does a process exist to determine which risk events to accept and which events to disregard?

380. What are key inputs and outputs of the software?

381. What is the BEST thing for the Hybrid Sharepoint project manager to do?

382. If you plan to take the PMP exam soon, what should you do to prepare?

383. Are measurement techniques employed to

determine the potential impact of proposed changes?

384. Who will provide inputs for it?

385. Have most organizations benefited from outsourcing?

386. Write a one to two-page paper describing your dream team for this Hybrid Sharepoint project. What type of people would you want on your team?

387. Is corrective action taken to bring Hybrid Sharepoint project performance into line with the Hybrid Sharepoint project plan?

388. What do you think the real problem was in this case?

389. Is the cost performance monitored to identify variances from the plan?

390. Do procedures exist describing how the Hybrid Sharepoint project scope will be managed?

391. What is wrong with this scenario?

2.18 Duration Estimating Worksheet: Hybrid Sharepoint

392. Is the Hybrid Sharepoint project responsive to community need?

393. What utility impacts are there?

394. What questions do you have?

395. Can the Hybrid Sharepoint project be constructed as planned?

396. What is cost and Hybrid Sharepoint project cost management?

397. How should ongoing costs be monitored to try to keep the Hybrid Sharepoint project within budget?

398. Will the Hybrid Sharepoint project collaborate with the local community and leverage resources?

399. Value pocket identification & quantification what are value pockets?

400. When does your organization expect to be able to complete it?

401. When, then?

402. Do any colleagues have experience with your organization and/or RFPs?

403. Science = process: remember the scientific method?

404. What is your role?

405. Done before proceeding with this activity or what can be done concurrently?

406. What is next?

407. What info is needed?

408. What is the total time required to complete the Hybrid Sharepoint project if no delays occur?

409. Small or large Hybrid Sharepoint project?

2.19 Project Schedule: Hybrid Sharepoint

410. Are procedures defined by which the Hybrid Sharepoint project schedule may be changed?

411. What is risk?

412. Did the Hybrid Sharepoint project come in on schedule?

413. Master Hybrid Sharepoint project schedule?

414. If there are any qualifying green components to this Hybrid Sharepoint project, what portion of the total Hybrid Sharepoint project cost is green?

415. What is the difference?

416. Did the Hybrid Sharepoint project come in under budget?

417. Schedule/cost recovery?

418. Are there activities that came from a template or previous Hybrid Sharepoint project that are not applicable on this phase of this Hybrid Sharepoint project?

419. Your best shot for providing estimations how complex/how much work does the activity require?

420. What is Hybrid Sharepoint project management?

421. Have all Hybrid Sharepoint project delays been adequately accounted for, communicated to all stakeholders and adjustments made in overall Hybrid Sharepoint project schedule?

422. Are quality inspections and review activities listed in the Hybrid Sharepoint project schedule(s)?

423. Why do you think schedule issues often cause the most conflicts on Hybrid Sharepoint projects?

424. Are the original Hybrid Sharepoint project schedule and budget realistic?

425. Why is software Hybrid Sharepoint project disaster so common?

426. Was the Hybrid Sharepoint project schedule reviewed by all stakeholders and formally accepted?

2.20 Cost Management Plan: Hybrid Sharepoint

427. Does the detailed work plan match the complexity of tasks with the capabilities of personnel?

428. Have process improvement efforts been completed before requirements efforts begin?

429. Are the Hybrid Sharepoint project plans updated on a frequent basis?

430. Have the reasons why the changes to your organizational systems and capabilities are required?

431. Environmental management – what changes in statutory environmental compliance requirements are anticipated during the Hybrid Sharepoint project?

432. Are adequate resources provided for the quality assurance function?

433. Are metrics used to evaluate and manage Vendors?

434. Are the payment terms being followed?

435. Risk Analysis?

436. Are staff skills known and available for each task?

437. Have lessons learned been conducted after each Hybrid Sharepoint project release?

438. Have Hybrid Sharepoint project management standards and procedures been identified / established and documented?

439. Does a documented Hybrid Sharepoint project organizational policy & plan (i.e. governance model) exist?

440. Hybrid Sharepoint project Objectives?

441. Are vendor contract reports, reviews and visits conducted periodically?

442. Is there a Steering Committee in place?

443. Time management – how will the schedule impact of changes be estimated and approved?

444. Are Hybrid Sharepoint project team members committed fulltime?

445. Are status reports received per the Hybrid Sharepoint project Plan?

2.21 Activity Cost Estimates: Hybrid Sharepoint

446. What is Hybrid Sharepoint project cost management?

447. What happens if you cannot produce the documentation for the single audit?

448. Were decisions made in a timely manner?

449. Specific - is the objective clear in terms of what, how, when, and where the situation will be changed?

450. Were sponsors and decision makers available when needed outside regularly scheduled meetings?

451. Does the activity use a common approach or business function to deliver its results?

452. How do you fund change orders?

453. Can you change your activities?

454. Were the costs or charges reasonable?

455. How do you allocate indirect costs to activities?

456. Why do you manage cost?

457. What were things that you did very well and want to do the same again on the next Hybrid Sharepoint project?

458. Does the estimator estimate by task or by person?

459. Which contract type places the most risk on the seller?

460. What are the audit requirements?

461. Were you satisfied with the work?

462. What is the Hybrid Sharepoint projects sustainability strategy that will ensure Hybrid Sharepoint project results will endure or be sustained?

463. In which phase of the acquisition process cycle does source qualifications reside?

2.22 Cost Estimating Worksheet: Hybrid Sharepoint

464. What additional Hybrid Sharepoint project(s) could be initiated as a result of this Hybrid Sharepoint project?

465. How will the results be shared and to whom?

466. What will others want?

467. Is it feasible to establish a control group arrangement?

468. Is the Hybrid Sharepoint project responsive to community need?

469. What is the estimated labor cost today based upon this information?

470. Who is best positioned to know and assist in identifying corresponding factors?

471. What happens to any remaining funds not used?

472. What is the purpose of estimating?

473. Does the Hybrid Sharepoint project provide innovative ways for stakeholders to overcome obstacles or deliver better outcomes?

474. Can a trend be established from historical performance data on the selected measure and are

the criteria for using trend analysis or forecasting methods met?

475. What can be included?

476. What costs are to be estimated?

477. Will the Hybrid Sharepoint project collaborate with the local community and leverage resources?

478. Ask: are others positioned to know, are others credible, and will others cooperate?

479. Identify the timeframe necessary to monitor progress and collect data to determine how the selected measure has changed?

2.23 Cost Baseline: Hybrid Sharepoint

480. Has the appropriate access to relevant data and analysis capability been granted?

481. How fast?

482. Should a more thorough impact analysis be conducted?

483. How likely is it to go wrong?

484. Pcs for your new business. what would the life cycle costs be?

485. Has the documentation relating to operation and maintenance of the product(s) or service(s) been delivered to, and accepted by, operations management?

486. Does it impact schedule, cost, quality?

487. Definition of done can be traced back to the definitions of what are you providing to the customer in terms of deliverables?

488. Have you identified skills that are missing from your team?

489. Are there contingencies or conditions related to the acceptance?

490. For what purpose ?

491. What do you want to measure?

492. What is the consequence?

493. Are you asking management for something as a result of this update?

494. Have all approved changes to the Hybrid Sharepoint project requirement been identified and impact on the performance, cost, and schedule baselines documented?

495. How do you manage cost?

496. Hybrid Sharepoint project goals -should others be reconsidered?

497. Who will use corresponding metrics?

498. On budget?

2.24 Quality Management Plan: Hybrid Sharepoint

499. Show/provide copy of procedures for taking field notes?

500. How does your organization determine the requirements and product/service features important to customers?

501. How many Hybrid Sharepoint project staff does this specific process affect?

502. What does it do for you (or to me)?

503. How is staff trained in procedures?

504. Diagrams and tables to account for complex concepts and increase overall readability?

505. Is there a Quality Management Plan?

506. How is staff trained?

507. Is there a procedure for this process?

508. Where do you focus?

509. With the five whys method, the team considers why the issue being explored occurred. do others then take that initial answer and ask why?

510. Meet how often?

511. Account for the procedures used to verify the data quality of the data being reviewed?

512. How does your organization maintain a safe and healthy work environment?

513. How do senior leaders create an environment that encourages learning and innovation?

514. Does a documented Hybrid Sharepoint project organizational policy & plan (i.e. governance model) exist?

515. How do you decide what information needs to be recorded?

516. What procedures are used to determine if you use, and the number of split, replicate or duplicate samples taken at a site?

517. How do you ensure that your sampling methods and procedures meet your data needs?

2.25 Quality Metrics: Hybrid Sharepoint

518. How can the effectiveness of each of the activities be measured?

519. How does one achieve stability?

520. Did evaluation start on time?

521. Is material complete (and does it meet the standards)?

522. What method of measurement do you use?

523. Are documents on hand to provide explanations of privacy and confidentiality?

524. How exactly do you define when differences exist?

525. What if the biggest risk to your business were the already stated people who do not complain?

526. What metrics are important and most beneficial to measure?

527. Should a modifier be included?

528. Do the operators focus on determining; is there anything you need to worry about?

529. How is it being measured?

530. What forces exist that would cause them to change?

531. Is quality culture a competitive advantage?

532. Where did complaints, returns and warranty claims come from?

533. What metrics do you measure?

534. Was material distributed on time?

535. Which data do others need in one place to target areas of improvement?

536. What percentage are outcome-based?

537. There are many reasons to shore up quality-related metrics, and what metrics are important?

2.26 Process Improvement Plan: Hybrid Sharepoint

538. What personnel are the coaches for your initiative?

539. Where do you want to be?

540. Does your process ensure quality?

541. Are there forms and procedures to collect and record the data?

542. What personnel are the sponsors for that initiative?

543. Who should prepare the process improvement action plan?

544. Management commitment at all levels?

545. Why do you want to achieve the goal?

546. Are you following the quality standards?

547. Modeling current processes is great, and will you ever see a return on that investment?

548. What personnel are the change agents for your initiative?

549. What actions are needed to address the problems and achieve the goals?

550. Have the frequency of collection and the points in the process where measurements will be made been determined?

551. Has the time line required to move measurement results from the points of collection to databases or users been established?

552. Have storage and access mechanisms and procedures been determined?

553. What lessons have you learned so far?

554. What makes people good SPI coaches?

555. How do you measure?

556. What is the test-cycle concept?

2.27 Responsibility Assignment Matrix: Hybrid Sharepoint

557. How do you assist them to be as productive as possible?

558. Are records maintained to show how undistributed budgets are controlled?

559. Do managers and team members provide helpful suggestions during review meetings?

560. Ideas for developing soft skills at your organization?

561. Will too many Communicating responsibilities tangle the Hybrid Sharepoint project in unnecessary communications?

562. Is cost and schedule performance measurement done in a consistent, systematic manner?

563. Do all the identified groups or people really need to be consulted?

564. Are material costs reported within the same period as that in which BCWP is earned for that material?

565. If a role has only Signing-off, or only Communicating responsibility and has no Performing, Accountable, or Monitoring responsibility, is it necessary?

566. Cwbs elements to be subcontracted, with identification of subcontractors?

567. Undistributed budgets, if any?

568. Incurrence of actual indirect costs in excess of budgets, by element of expense?

569. The already stated responsible for the establishment of budgets and assignment of resources for overhead performance?

570. Will too many Signing-off responsibilities delay the completion of the activity/deliverable?

571. Does the accounting system provide a basis for auditing records of direct costs chargeable to the contract?

572. How can this help you with team building?

573. What do you do when people do not respond?

574. What is the primary purpose of the human resource plan?

2.28 Roles and Responsibilities: Hybrid Sharepoint

575. Where are you most strong as a supervisor?

576. What areas would you highlight for changes or improvements?

577. Required skills, knowledge, experience?

578. What specific behaviors did you observe?

579. Is there a training program in place for stakeholders covering expectations, roles and responsibilities and any addition knowledge others need to be good stakeholders?

580. How well did the Hybrid Sharepoint project Team understand the expectations of specific roles and responsibilities?

581. Are Hybrid Sharepoint project team roles and responsibilities identified and documented?

582. What should you do now to ensure that you are meeting all expectations of your current position?

583. Key conclusions and recommendations: Are conclusions and recommendations relevant and acceptable?

584. What is working well?

585. Are governance roles and responsibilities documented?

586. What should you do now to prepare for your career 5+ years from now?

587. What expectations were met?

588. Who is involved?

589. Attainable / achievable: the goal is attainable; can you actually accomplish the goal?

590. Implementation of actions: Who are the responsible units?

591. What should you do now to prepare yourself for a promotion, increased responsibilities or a different job?

592. Once the responsibilities are defined for the Hybrid Sharepoint project, have the deliverables, roles and responsibilities been clearly communicated to every participant?

593. What are your major roles and responsibilities in the area of performance measurement and assessment?

2.29 Human Resource Management Plan: Hybrid Sharepoint

594. How will the Hybrid Sharepoint project manage expectations & meet needs and requirements?

595. Are people motivated to meet the current and future challenges?

596. Are written status reports provided on a designated frequent basis?

597. Is there an onboarding process in place?

598. Is there a formal process for updating the Hybrid Sharepoint project baseline?

599. Identify who is needed on the core Hybrid Sharepoint project team to complete Hybrid Sharepoint project deliverables and achieve its goals and objectives. What skills, knowledge and experiences are required?

600. Are quality metrics defined?

601. Have the key elements of a coherent Hybrid Sharepoint project management strategy been established?

602. How relevant is this attribute to this Hybrid Sharepoint project or audit?

603. Are the key elements of a Hybrid Sharepoint

project Charter present?

604. Has a Hybrid Sharepoint project Communications Plan been developed?

605. Is the communication plan being followed?

606. Does the schedule include Hybrid Sharepoint project management time and change request analysis time?

607. Are changes in deliverable commitments agreed to by all affected groups & individuals?

2.30 Communications Management Plan: Hybrid Sharepoint

608. Is there an important stakeholder who is actively opposed and will not receive messages?

609. What is the stakeholders level of authority?

610. Are others part of the communications management plan?

611. Who did you turn to if you had questions?

612. What help do you and your team need from the stakeholder?

613. Who to share with?

614. Who are the members of the governing body?

615. Who is involved as you identify stakeholders?

616. Which team member will work with each stakeholder?

617. Are you constantly rushing from meeting to meeting?

618. Conflict resolution -which method when?

619. Why is stakeholder engagement important?

620. Who were proponents/opponents?

621. How did the term stakeholder originate?

622. Are there too many who have an interest in some aspect of your work?

623. What communications method?

624. Are the stakeholders getting the information others need, are others consulted, are concerns addressed?

625. Do you feel more overwhelmed by stakeholders?

626. Do you ask; can you recommend others for you to talk with about this initiative?

2.31 Risk Management Plan: Hybrid Sharepoint

627. Technology risk: is the Hybrid Sharepoint project technically feasible?

628. What will the damage be?

629. Do the requirements require the creation of components that are unlike anything your organization has previously built?

630. What is the probability the risk avoidance strategy will be successful?

631. Are the reports useful and easy to read?

632. Is the customer willing to establish rapid communication links with the developer?

633. What does a risk management program do?

634. Are the metrics meaningful and useful?

635. Prioritized components/features?

636. Are testing tools available and suitable?

637. Who should be notified of the occurrence of each of the indicators?

638. Are status updates being made on schedule and are the updates clearly described?

639. Is the customer willing to participate in reviews?

640. Market risk: will the new product be useful to your organization or marketable to others?

641. What would you do?

642. Which risks should get the attention?

643. Who has experience with this?

644. What can go wrong?

645. Degree of confidence in estimated size estimate?

646. Is security a central objective?

2.32 Risk Register: Hybrid Sharepoint

647. What is the probability and impact of the risk occurring?

648. What evidence do you have to justify the likelihood score of the risk (audit, incident report, claim, complaints, inspection, internal review)?

649. What is a Community Risk Register?

650. Assume the risk event or situation happens, what would the impact be?

651. Methodology: how will risk management be performed on this Hybrid Sharepoint project?

652. What are the major risks facing the Hybrid Sharepoint project?

653. Assume the event happens, what is the Most Likely impact?

654. How are risks graded?

655. How could corresponding Risk affect the Hybrid Sharepoint project in terms of cost and schedule?

656. Are corrective measures implemented as planned?

657. When will it happen?

658. What may happen or not go according to plan?

659. Preventative actions - planned actions to reduce the likelihood a risk will occur and/or reduce the seriousness should it occur. What should you do now?

660. Amongst the action plans and recommendations that you have to introduce are there some that could stop or delay the overall program?

661. What is your current and future risk profile?

662. Who needs to know about this?

663. What are the main aims, objectives of the policy, strategy, or service and the intended outcomes?

664. Are there any knock-on effects/impact on any of the other areas?

665. Risk documentation: what reporting formats and processes will be used for risk management activities?

2.33 Probability and Impact Assessment: Hybrid Sharepoint

666. Is the process supported by tools?

667. What are the likely future requirements?

668. Is it necessary to deeply assess all Hybrid Sharepoint project risks?

669. What should be the external organizations responsibility vis-à-vis total stake in the Hybrid Sharepoint project?

670. Will there be an increase in the political conservatism?

671. What should be the requirement of organizational restructuring as each subHybrid Sharepoint project goes through a different lifecycle phase?

672. Are there new risks that mitigation strategies might introduce?

673. How are you working with risks?

674. Have staff received necessary training?

675. Is the number of people on the Hybrid Sharepoint project team adequate to do the job?

676. What are the current demands of the customer?

677. Do you use diagramming techniques to show cause and effect?

678. Are requirements fully understood by the software engineering team and customers?

679. Is the delay in one subHybrid Sharepoint project going to affect another?

680. What are the chances the event will occur?

681. How will economic events and trends likely affect the Hybrid Sharepoint project?

682. Is the technology to be built new to your organization?

683. What should be done with non-critical risks?

684. Workarounds are determined during which step of risk management?

685. What is the likelihood of a breakthrough?

2.34 Probability and Impact Matrix: Hybrid Sharepoint

686. How are risks and risk management perceived in the Hybrid Sharepoint project?

687. What action do you usually take against risks?

688. What can possibly go wrong?

689. What will be the impact or consequence if the risk occurs?

690. What do you expect?

691. Which of your Hybrid Sharepoint projects should be selected when compared with other Hybrid Sharepoint projects?

692. Costs associated with late delivery or a defective product?

693. Workarounds are determined during which risk management process?

694. Have customers been involved fully in the definition of requirements?

695. Can you avoid altogether some things that might go wrong?

696. How well is the risk understood?

697. What are the channels available for distribution to the customer?

698. Is there any sign of biased ranking?

699. What is the probability of the risk occurring?

700. Brain storm – mind maps, what if?

701. Do requirements demand the use of new analysis, design, or testing methods?

2.35 Risk Data Sheet: Hybrid Sharepoint

702. What if client refuses?

703. Type of risk identified?

704. Risk of what?

705. Whom do you serve (customers)?

706. Has the most cost-effective solution been chosen?

707. Has a sensitivity analysis been carried out?

708. If it happens, what are the consequences?

709. What will be the consequences if it happens?

710. Are new hazards created?

711. What is the environment within which you operate (social trends, economic, community values, broad based participation, national directions etc.)?

712. How do you handle product safely?

713. What actions can be taken to eliminate or remove risk?

714. Will revised controls lead to tolerable risk levels?

715. How reliable is the data source?

716. What do you know?

717. What are you weak at and therefore need to do better?

718. Potential for recurrence?

719. What are the main opportunities available to you that you should grab while you can?

720. What are you trying to achieve (Objectives)?

2.36 Procurement Management Plan: Hybrid Sharepoint

721. Are the Hybrid Sharepoint project plans updated on a frequent basis?

722. Are target dates established for each milestone deliverable?

723. Was an original risk assessment/risk management plan completed?

724. Are multiple estimation methods being employed?

725. Does the Hybrid Sharepoint project have a Statement of Work?

726. What were things that you did very well and want to do the same again on the next Hybrid Sharepoint project?

727. Are the key elements of a Hybrid Sharepoint project Charter present?

728. Is the steering committee active in Hybrid Sharepoint project oversight?

729. Has the Hybrid Sharepoint project scope been baselined?

730. How will multiple providers be managed?

731. Are the appropriate IT resources adequate to meet planned commitments?

732. Is there a set of procedures defining the scope, procedures, and deliverables defining quality control?

733. Have key stakeholders been identified?

734. What are your quality assurance overheads?

735. Have stakeholder accountabilities & responsibilities been clearly defined?

736. Have the key elements of a coherent Hybrid Sharepoint project management strategy been established?

737. Are trade-offs between accepting the risk and mitigating the risk identified?

2.37 Source Selection Criteria: Hybrid Sharepoint

738. What documentation is needed for a tradeoff decision?

739. Is the offeror pricing what is technically proposed?

740. What information is to be provided and when should it be provided?

741. What evidence should be provided regarding proposal evaluations?

742. Has all proposal data been loaded?

743. What instructions should be provided regarding oral presentations?

744. What are the guiding principles for developing an evaluation report?

745. Is a cost realism analysis used?

746. In the technical/management area, what criteria do you use to determine the final evaluation ratings?

747. What procedures are followed when a contractor requires access to classified information or a significant quantity of special material/information?

748. Have team members been adequately trained?

749. When is it appropriate to issue a Draft Request for Proposal (DRFP)?

750. What aspects should the contracting officer brief the Hybrid Sharepoint project on prior to evaluation of proposals?

751. What is the basis of an estimate and what assumptions were made?

752. Do you want to have them collaborate at subfactor level?

753. How should the oral presentations be handled?

754. What risks were identified in the proposals?

755. What common questions or problems are associated with debriefings?

756. Are there any specific considerations that precludes offers from being selected as the awardee?

2.38 Stakeholder Management Plan: Hybrid Sharepoint

757. Who is responsible for the post implementation review process?

758. What is the difference between product and Hybrid Sharepoint project scope?

759. What is the process for purchases that arent acceptable (eg damaged goods)?

760. Do any protocols apply for records management?

761. How accurate and complete is the information?

762. Are there any potential occupational health and safety issues due to the proposed purchases?

763. What training requirements are there based upon the required skills and resources?

764. What preventative action can be taken to reduce the likelihood a risk will be realised?

765. Are all resource assumptions documented?

766. Does this include subcontracted development?

767. What has to be purchased?

768. Does the system design reflect the requirements?

769. Are there ways to reduce the time it takes to get something approved?

770. Are there nonconformance issues?

771. Contradictory information between different documents?

772. Are action items captured and managed?

773. Which impacts could serve as impediments?

2.39 Change Management Plan: Hybrid Sharepoint

774. What are the major changes to processes?

775. What policies and procedures need to be changed?

776. Identify the current level of skills and knowledge and behaviours of the group that will be impacted on. What prerequisite knowledge do corresponding groups need?

777. Do you need a new organizational structure?

778. What are the training strategies?

779. Change invariability confront many relationships especially the already stated that require a set of behaviours What roles with in your organization are affected and how?

780. What new behaviours are required?

781. Have the approved procedures and policies been published?

782. Is there an adequate supply of people for the new roles?

783. What would be an estimate of the total cost for the activities required to carry out the change initiative?

784. Has the relevant business unit been notified of installation and support requirements?

785. What prerequisite knowledge do corresponding groups need?

786. Will the culture embrace or reject this change?

787. Do you need a new organization structure?

788. What are the specific target groups/audiences that will be impacted by this change?

789. What is the negative impact of communicating too soon or too late?

3.0 Executing Process Group: Hybrid Sharepoint

790. How could stakeholders negatively impact your Hybrid Sharepoint project?

791. When will the Hybrid Sharepoint project be done?

792. It under budget or over budget?

793. Who will provide training?

794. How does the job market and current state of the economy affect human resource management?

795. Does the Hybrid Sharepoint project team have enough people to execute the Hybrid Sharepoint project plan?

796. Are decisions made in a timely manner?

797. How could you control progress of your Hybrid Sharepoint project?

798. What areas does the group agree are the biggest success on the Hybrid Sharepoint project?

799. What are the typical Hybrid Sharepoint project management skills?

800. How do you measure difficulty?

801. Is the schedule for the set products being met?

802. Could a new application negatively affect the current IT infrastructure?

803. How does Hybrid Sharepoint project management relate to other disciplines?

804. Do schedule issues conflicts?

805. What are the critical steps involved in selecting measures and initiatives?

806. How will you avoid scope creep?

807. Who are the Hybrid Sharepoint project stakeholders?

808. Would you rate yourself as being risk-averse, risk-neutral, or risk-seeking?

809. After how many days will the lease cost be the same as the purchase cost for the equipment?

3.1 Team Member Status Report: Hybrid Sharepoint

810. How much risk is involved?

811. Is there evidence that staff is taking a more professional approach toward management of your organizations Hybrid Sharepoint projects?

812. Does every department have to have a Hybrid Sharepoint project Manager on staff?

813. The problem with Reward & Recognition Programs is that the truly deserving people all too often get left out. How can you make it practical?

814. How it is to be done?

815. Are the attitudes of staff regarding Hybrid Sharepoint project work improving?

816. Will the staff do training or is that done by a third party?

817. When a teams productivity and success depend on collaboration and the efficient flow of information, what generally fails them?

818. How does this product, good, or service meet the needs of the Hybrid Sharepoint project and your organization as a whole?

819. Does the product, good, or service already exist

within your organization?

820. How can you make it practical?

821. Does your organization have the means (staff, money, contract, etc.) to produce or to acquire the product, good, or service?

822. Are the products of your organizations Hybrid Sharepoint projects meeting customers objectives?

823. How will resource planning be done?

824. Why is it to be done?

825. Are your organizations Hybrid Sharepoint projects more successful over time?

826. What is to be done?

827. What specific interest groups do you have in place?

828. Do you have an Enterprise Hybrid Sharepoint project Management Office (EPMO)?

3.2 Change Request: Hybrid Sharepoint

829. When do you create a change request?

830. Who is responsible to authorize changes?

831. Who will perform the change?

832. What are the duties of the change control team?

833. How do team members communicate with each other?

834. Will there be a change request form in use?

835. Customer acceptance plan how will the customer verify the change has been implemented successfully?

836. Who is included in the change control team?

837. What is the function of the change control committee?

838. What is the relationship between requirements attributes and attributes like complexity and size?

839. How are changes graded and who is responsible for the rating?

840. How are changes requested (forms, method of communication)?

841. How is the change documented (format, content, storage)?

842. Are change requests logged and managed?

843. Who is responsible for the implementation and monitoring of all measures?

844. How shall the implementation of changes be recorded?

845. Will all change requests and current status be logged?

846. Since there are no change requests in your Hybrid Sharepoint project at this point, what must you have before you begin?

847. Does the schedule include Hybrid Sharepoint project management time and change request analysis time?

3.3 Change Log: Hybrid Sharepoint

848. Is the change request open, closed or pending?

849. Does the suggested change request represent a desired enhancement to the products functionality?

850. Do the described changes impact on the integrity or security of the system?

851. Is the change backward compatible without limitations?

852. Does the suggested change request seem to represent a necessary enhancement to the product?

853. Will the Hybrid Sharepoint project fail if the change request is not executed?

854. Is the change request within Hybrid Sharepoint project scope?

855. How does this change affect scope?

856. Is the submitted change a new change or a modification of a previously approved change?

857. Is this a mandatory replacement?

858. Where do changes come from?

859. Is the requested change request a result of changes in other Hybrid Sharepoint project(s)?

860. When was the request approved?

861. How does this relate to the standards developed for specific business processes?

862. When was the request submitted?

863. How does this change affect the timeline of the schedule?

864. Who initiated the change request?

3.4 Decision Log: Hybrid Sharepoint

865. Who will be given a copy of this document and where will it be kept?

866. With whom was the decision shared or considered?

867. What is your overall strategy for quality control / quality assurance procedures?

868. What is the average size of your matters in an applicable measurement?

869. Is everything working as expected?

870. How does provision of information, both in terms of content and presentation, influence acceptance of alternative strategies?

871. At what point in time does loss become unacceptable?

872. Meeting purpose; why does this team meet?

873. Linked to original objective?

874. Decision-making process; how will the team make decisions?

875. How do you know when you are achieving it?

876. What makes you different or better than others companies selling the same thing?

877. How do you define success?

878. How effective is maintaining the log at facilitating organizational learning?

879. It becomes critical to track and periodically revisit both operational effectiveness; Are you noticing all that you need to, and are you interpreting what you see effectively?

880. What eDiscovery problem or issue did your organization set out to fix or make better?

881. Does anything need to be adjusted?

882. Which variables make a critical difference?

883. How does the use a Decision Support System influence the strategies/tactics or costs?

884. How consolidated and comprehensive a story can you tell by capturing currently available incident data in a central location and through a log of key decisions during an incident?

3.5 Quality Audit: Hybrid Sharepoint

885. How does your organization know that its system for inducting new staff to maximize workplace contributions are appropriately effective and constructive?

886. Has a written procedure been established to identify devices during all stages of receipt, reconditioning, distribution and installation so that mix-ups are prevented?

887. Are storage areas and reconditioning operations designed to prevent mix-ups and assure orderly handling of both the distressed and reconditioned devices?

888. How does your organization know that its security arrangements are appropriately effective and constructive?

889. How does your organization know that it is effectively and constructively guiding staff through to timely completion of tasks?

890. How does your organization know that its system for attending to the health and wellbeing of its staff is appropriately effective and constructive?

891. What are your supplier audits?

892. What does the organizarion look for in a Quality audit?

893. For each device to be reconditioned, are device specifications, such as appropriate engineering drawings, component specifications and software specifications, maintained?

894. What happens if your organization fails its Quality Audit?

895. Are all employees including salespersons made aware that they must report all complaints received from any source for inclusion in the complaint handling system?

896. How does your organization know that the support for its staff is appropriately effective and constructive?

897. Are the intentions consistent with external obligations (such as applicable laws)?

898. How does your organization know that its policy management system is appropriately effective and constructive?

899. How do you indicate the extent to which your personnel would be expected to contribute to the work effort?

900. How are you auditing your organizations compliance with regulations?

901. Do the suppliers use a formal quality system?

902. Have the risks associated with the intentions been identified, analyzed and appropriate responses developed?

903. How does your organization know that its staff placements are appropriately effective and constructive in relation to program-related learning outcomes?

904. Does the suppliers quality system have a written procedure for corrective action when a defect occurs?

3.6 Team Directory: Hybrid Sharepoint

905. How do unidentified risks impact the outcome of the Hybrid Sharepoint project?

906. Process decisions: how well was task order work performed?

907. Process decisions: do job conditions warrant additional actions to collect job information and document on-site activity?

908. Decisions: what could be done better to improve the quality of the constructed product?

909. Does a Hybrid Sharepoint project team directory list all resources assigned to the Hybrid Sharepoint project?

910. How and in what format should information be presented?

911. When does information need to be distributed?

912. Process decisions: are there any statutory or regulatory issues relevant to the timely execution of work?

913. Contract requirements complied with?

914. How will the team handle changes?

915. How does the team resolve conflicts and ensure tasks are completed?

916. Have you decided when to celebrate the Hybrid Sharepoint projects completion date?

917. Who will report Hybrid Sharepoint project status to all stakeholders?

918. How will you accomplish and manage the objectives?

919. Who are the Team Members?

920. Who will write the meeting minutes and distribute?

921. Who should receive information (all stakeholders)?

3.7 Team Operating Agreement: Hybrid Sharepoint

922. What administrative supports will be put in place to support the team and the teams supervisor?

923. Must your members collaborate successfully to complete Hybrid Sharepoint projects?

924. Did you delegate tasks such as taking meeting minutes, presenting a topic and soliciting input?

925. Resource allocation: how will individual team members account for time and expenses, and how will this be allocated in the team budget?

926. What individual strengths does each team member bring to the group?

927. To whom do you deliver your services?

928. The method to be used in the decision making process; Will it be consensus, majority rule, or the supervisor having the final say?

929. Do team members need to frequently communicate as a full group to make timely decisions?

930. Do you solicit member feedback about meetings and what would make them better?

931. Are leadership responsibilities shared among

team members (versus a single leader)?

932. Methodologies: how will key team processes be implemented, such as training, research, work deliverable production, review and approval processes, knowledge management, and meeting procedures?

933. Did you recap the meeting purpose, time, and expectations?

934. Do you vary your voice pace, tone and pitch to engage participants and gain involvement?

935. Confidentiality: how will confidential information be handled?

936. Do you upload presentation materials in advance and test the technology?

937. Have you established procedures that team members can follow to work effectively together, such as a team operating agreement?

938. Are there influences outside the team that may affect performance, and if so, have you identified and addressed them?

939. Do you send out the agenda and meeting materials in advance?

940. How will you resolve conflict efficiently and respectfully?

941. What are the safety issues/risks that need to be addressed and/or that the team needs to consider?

3.8 Team Performance Assessment: Hybrid Sharepoint

942. To what degree are the goals ambitious?

943. Which situations call for a more extreme type of adaptiveness in which team members actually re-define roles?

944. To what degree will the team ensure that all members equitably share the work essential to the success of the team?

945. To what degree does the teams purpose constitute a broader, deeper aspiration than just accomplishing short-term goals?

946. Do friends perform better than acquaintances?

947. How hard did you try to make a good selection?

948. To what degree can all members engage in open and interactive considerations?

949. How do you encourage members to learn from each other?

950. To what degree does the team possess adequate membership to achieve its ends?

951. Can team performance be reliably measured in simulator and live exercises using the same assessment tool?

952. Do you promptly inform members about major developments that may affect them?

953. To what degree will the team adopt a concrete, clearly understood, and agreed-upon approach that will result in achievement of the teams goals?

954. To what degree do team members articulate the teams work approach?

955. Where to from here?

956. To what degree does the teams approach to its work allow for modification and improvement over time?

957. What are you doing specifically to develop the leaders around you?

958. To what degree does the teams purpose contain themes that are particularly meaningful and memorable?

959. To what degree do team members understand one anothers roles and skills?

960. What are teams?

961. Individual task proficiency and team process behavior: what is important for team functioning?

3.9 Team Member Performance Assessment: Hybrid Sharepoint

962. What future plans (e.g., modifications) do you have for your program?

963. How will they be formed?

964. How do you make use of research?

965. What entity leads the process, selects a potential restructuring option and develops the plan?

966. How do you start collaborating?

967. To what degree are the goals realistic?

968. Does statute or regulation require the job responsibility?

969. How do you know that all team members are learning?

970. Who they are?

971. To what extent did the evaluation influence the instructional path, such as with adaptive testing?

972. How is the timing of assessments organized (e.g., pre/post-test, single point during training, multiple reassessment during training)?

973. What does collaboration look like?

974. To what degree will new and supplemental skills be introduced as the need is recognized?

975. What makes them effective?

976. What are the basic principles and objectives of performance measurement and assessment?

977. Can your organization rate by exception and assume that most employees are performing at an acceptable level?

978. To what degree is the team cognizant of small wins to be celebrated along the way?

979. What stakeholders must be involved in the development and oversight of the performance plan?

3.10 Issue Log: Hybrid Sharepoint

980. Which stakeholders are thought leaders, influences, or early adopters?

981. Is access to the Issue Log controlled?

982. In your work, how much time is spent on stakeholder identification?

983. What help do you and your team need from the stakeholders?

984. What are the typical contents?

985. Who is the issue assigned to?

986. In classifying stakeholders, which approach to do so are you using?

987. Is the issue log kept in a safe place?

988. What does the stakeholder need from the team?

989. What approaches do you use?

990. Persistence; will users learn a work around or will they be bothered every time?

991. What is the impact on the risks?

992. Why do you manage communications?

993. Who reported the issue?

994. Who do you turn to if you have questions?

995. Do you have members of your team responsible for certain stakeholders?

996. Who have you worked with in past, similar initiatives?

4.0 Monitoring and Controlling Process Group: Hybrid Sharepoint

997. What resources are necessary?

998. Are the services being delivered?

999. How many potential communications channels exist on the Hybrid Sharepoint project?

1000. In what way has the program come up with innovative measures for problem-solving?

1001. How will staff learn how to use the deliverables?

1002. What departments are involved in its daily operation?

1003. Accuracy: what design will lead to accurate information?

1004. How is agile program management done?

1005. How well did the chosen processes produce the expected results?

1006. How is Agile Hybrid Sharepoint project Management done?

1007. Who needs to be engaged upfront to ensure use of results?

1008. What were things that you did very well and

want to do the same again on the next Hybrid Sharepoint project?

1009. Change, where should you look for problems?

1010. If a risk event occurs, what will you do?

1011. How were collaborations developed, and how are they sustained?

1012. How do you monitor progress?

1013. What good practices or successful experiences or transferable examples have been identified?

1014. Is there undesirable impact on staff or resources?

4.1 Project Performance Report: Hybrid Sharepoint

1015. To what degree does the teams work approach provide opportunity for members to engage in fact-based problem solving?

1016. To what degree can team members vigorously define the teams purpose in considerations with others who are not part of the functioning team?

1017. To what degree are the tasks requirements reflected in the flow and storage of information?

1018. To what degree does the formal organization make use of individual resources and meet individual needs?

1019. What is the PRS?

1020. To what degree are the skill areas critical to team performance present?

1021. To what degree do team members frequently explore the teams purpose and its implications?

1022. What is the degree to which rules govern information exchange between groups?

1023. To what degree do the structures of the formal organization motivate taskrelevant behavior and facilitate task completion?

1024. What degree are the relative importance and priority of the goals clear to all team members?

1025. To what degree do the goals specify concrete team work products?

1026. How will procurement be coordinated with other Hybrid Sharepoint project aspects, such as scheduling and performance reporting?

1027. To what degree do team members agree with the goals, relative importance, and the ways in which achievement will be measured?

1028. To what degree are the structures of the formal organization consistent with the behaviors in the informal organization?

1029. To what degree are the demands of the task compatible with and converge with the relationships of the informal organization?

1030. To what degree do all members feel responsible for all agreed-upon measures?

4.2 Variance Analysis: Hybrid Sharepoint

1031. Are there externalities from having some customers, even if they are unprofitable in the short run?

1032. Did a new competitor enter the market?

1033. What is the actual cost of work performed?

1034. Contemplated overhead expenditure for each period based on the best information currently is available?

1035. Does the contractor use objective results, design reviews and tests to trace schedule performance?

1036. What is the incurrence of actual indirect costs in excess of budgets, by element of expense?

1037. How does your organization allocate the cost of shared expenses and services?

1038. Is all contract work included in the CWBS?

1039. Does the contractors system identify work accomplishment against the schedule plan?

1040. Why do variances exist?

1041. How are material, labor, and overhead standards

set?

1042. What business event causes fluctuations?

1043. How do you evaluate the impact of schedule changes, work around, et?

1044. Are there changes in the direct base to which overhead costs are allocated?

1045. Are the actual costs used for variance analysis reconcilable with data from the accounting system?

1046. The anticipated business volume?

1047. How does your organization measure performance?

1048. Is the anticipated (firm and potential) business base Hybrid Sharepoint projected in a rational, consistent manner?

1049. Are authorized changes being incorporated in a timely manner?

4.3 Earned Value Status: Hybrid Sharepoint

1050. Where are your problem areas?

1051. Are you hitting your Hybrid Sharepoint projects targets?

1052. When is it going to finish?

1053. Earned value can be used in almost any Hybrid Sharepoint project situation and in almost any Hybrid Sharepoint project environment. it may be used on large Hybrid Sharepoint projects, medium sized Hybrid Sharepoint projects, tiny Hybrid Sharepoint projects (in cut-down form), complex and simple Hybrid Sharepoint projects and in any market sector. some people, of course, know all about earned value, they have used it for years - but perhaps not as effectively as they could have?

1054. How does this compare with other Hybrid Sharepoint projects?

1055. If earned value management (EVM) is so good in determining the true status of a Hybrid Sharepoint project and Hybrid Sharepoint project its completion, why is it that hardly any one uses it in information systems related Hybrid Sharepoint projects?

1056. Verification is a process of ensuring that the developed system satisfies the stakeholders agreements and specifications; Are you building the product right? What do you verify?

1057. What is the unit of forecast value?

1058. Where is evidence-based earned value in your organization reported?

1059. Validation is a process of ensuring that the developed system will actually achieve the stakeholders desired outcomes; Are you building the right product? What do you validate?

1060. How much is it going to cost by the finish?

4.4 Risk Audit: Hybrid Sharepoint

1061. What are the costs associated with late delivery or a defective product?

1062. From an empirical perspective, does the business risk approach lead to a more effective audit, or simply to increased consulting revenue detrimental to audit rigor?

1063. Tradeoff: how much risk can be tolerated and still deliver the products where they need to be?

1064. Auditor independence: a burdensome constraint or a core value?

1065. Do you have financial policies and procedures in place to guide officers of your organization/treasurer/general members?

1066. Is risk an management agenda item?

1067. What can be measured?

1068. Do you have an emergency plan?

1069. Are all programs planned and conducted according to recognized safety standards?

1070. What is the anticipated volatility of the requirements?

1071. How are risk appetites expressed?

1072. What does your data tell you about your risks?

1073. Do you have position descriptions for all key paid and volunteer positions in your organization?

1074. Do you have position descriptions for all office bearers/staff?

1075. Does the adoption of a business risk audit approach change internal control documentation and testing practices?

1076. When your organization is entering into a major contract, does it seek legal advice?

1077. If applicable; which route/packaging option do you choose for transport of hazmat material?

1078. Do you have a procedure for dealing with complaints?

1079. Do industry specialists and business risk auditors enhance audit reporting accuracy?

1080. How effective are your risk controls?

4.5 Contractor Status Report: Hybrid Sharepoint

1081. How long have you been using the services?

1082. Describe how often regular updates are made to the proposed solution. Are corresponding regular updates included in the standard maintenance plan?

1083. Are there contractual transfer concerns?

1084. How is risk transferred?

1085. What was the overall budget or estimated cost?

1086. What are the minimum and optimal bandwidth requirements for the proposed solution?

1087. What is the average response time for answering a support call?

1088. How does the proposed individual meet each requirement?

1089. What was the budget or estimated cost for your organizations services?

1090. If applicable; describe your standard schedule for new software version releases. Are new software version releases included in the standard maintenance plan?

1091. Who can list a Hybrid Sharepoint project as

organization experience, your organization or a previous employee of your organization?

1092. What process manages the contracts?

1093. What was the actual budget or estimated cost for your organizations services?

1094. What was the final actual cost?

4.6 Formal Acceptance: Hybrid Sharepoint

1095. Was the Hybrid Sharepoint project goal achieved?

1096. What lessons were learned about your Hybrid Sharepoint project management methodology?

1097. Was the client satisfied with the Hybrid Sharepoint project results?

1098. Does it do what client said it would?

1099. Do you buy pre-configured systems or build your own configuration?

1100. General estimate of the costs and times to complete the Hybrid Sharepoint project?

1101. Was business value realized?

1102. Was the Hybrid Sharepoint project managed well?

1103. What is the Acceptance Management Process?

1104. Who would use it?

1105. Is formal acceptance of the Hybrid Sharepoint project product documented and distributed?

1106. Did the Hybrid Sharepoint project manager and

team act in a professional and ethical manner?

1107. Was the sponsor/customer satisfied?

1108. How well did the team follow the methodology?

1109. What can you do better next time?

1110. Do you buy-in installation services?

1111. Does it do what Hybrid Sharepoint project team said it would?

1112. What are the requirements against which to test, Who will execute?

1113. Do you perform formal acceptance or burn-in tests?

1114. Have all comments been addressed?

5.0 Closing Process Group: Hybrid Sharepoint

1115. What were the desired outcomes?

1116. What areas were overlooked on this Hybrid Sharepoint project?

1117. Contingency planning. if a risk event occurs, what will you do?

1118. What will you do to minimize the impact should a risk event occur?

1119. Was the user/client satisfied with the end product?

1120. Will the Hybrid Sharepoint project deliverable(s) replace a current asset or group of assets?

1121. Is this a follow-on to a previous Hybrid Sharepoint project?

1122. Is this an updated Hybrid Sharepoint project Proposal Document?

1123. Did the Hybrid Sharepoint project management methodology work?

1124. How critical is the Hybrid Sharepoint project success to the success of your organization?

1125. Is the Hybrid Sharepoint project funded?

1126. How well defined and documented were the Hybrid Sharepoint project management processes you chose to use?

1127. What could have been improved?

1128. What will you do?

1129. Were risks identified and mitigated?

1130. Was the schedule met?

5.1 Procurement Audit: Hybrid Sharepoint

1131. Are there mechanisms in place to evaluate the performance of the departments suppliers?

1132. Are all mutilated and voided checks retained for proper accounting of pre-numbered checks?

1133. Was confidentiality ensured when necessary?

1134. Do appropriate controls ensure that procurement decisions are not biased by conflicts of interest or corruption?

1135. Was the estimated contract value in line with the final cost of the contract awarded?

1136. Are there authorizations on file to support all deductions from payroll checks?

1137. Does the contract include performance-based clauses?

1138. Is the issuance of purchase orders scheduled so that orders are not issued daily?

1139. Have guidelines incorporating the principles and objectives of a robust procurement practice been established?

1140. Does the strategy ensure that the concepts of standardisation and coordination of procurement are used to take advantage of the departments collective buying power?

1141. Are the internal control systems operational?

1142. Was the chosen procedure the most efficient and effective for the performance of the contract?

1143. Has the expected benefits from realisation of the procurement Hybrid Sharepoint project been calculated?

1144. Are the right skills, experiences and competencies present in the acquisition workgroup and are the necessary outside specialists involved in part of the process?

1145. Is the procurement Hybrid Sharepoint project efficiently managed?

1146. Has the department identified and described the different elements in the procurement process?

1147. Is data securely stored?

1148. Are eu procurement regulations applicable?

1149. Did the chosen procedure ensure competition and transparency?

1150. Does the strategy discus the best manner of purchase, considering the types of goods and services needed?

5.2 Contract Close-Out: Hybrid Sharepoint

1151. Have all contracts been completed?

1152. Was the contract sufficiently clear so as not to result in numerous disputes and misunderstandings?

1153. Why Outsource?

1154. Has each contract been audited to verify acceptance and delivery?

1155. Change in circumstances?

1156. Are the signers the authorized officials?

1157. Change in attitude or behavior?

1158. Have all acceptance criteria been met prior to final payment to contractors?

1159. Have all contracts been closed?

1160. Have all contract records been included in the Hybrid Sharepoint project archives?

1161. How is the contracting office notified of the automatic contract close-out?

1162. What happens to the recipient of services?

1163. How/when used ?

1164. Parties: Authorized?

1165. Parties: who is involved?

1166. What is capture management?

1167. Was the contract complete without requiring numerous changes and revisions?

1168. Change in knowledge?

1169. How does it work?

1170. Was the contract type appropriate?

5.3 Project or Phase Close-Out: Hybrid Sharepoint

1171. Who controlled key decisions that were made?

1172. Were the outcomes different from the already stated planned?

1173. In preparing the Lessons Learned report, should it reflect a consensus viewpoint, or should the report reflect the different individual viewpoints?

1174. Does the lesson describe a function that would be done differently the next time?

1175. Did the Hybrid Sharepoint project management methodology work?

1176. What are they?

1177. How much influence did the stakeholder have over others?

1178. Planned completion date?

1179. Have business partners been involved extensively, and what data was required for them?

1180. Does the lesson educate others to improve performance?

1181. Complete yes or no?

1182. Were messages directly related to the release strategy or phases of the Hybrid Sharepoint project?

1183. What security considerations needed to be addressed during the procurement life cycle?

1184. What were the goals and objectives of the communications strategy for the Hybrid Sharepoint project?

1185. What was expected from each stakeholder?

1186. What was the preferred delivery mechanism?

1187. What information did each stakeholder need to contribute to the Hybrid Sharepoint projects success?

1188. What could be done to improve the process?

1189. Who are the Hybrid Sharepoint project stakeholders and what are roles and involvement?

5.4 Lessons Learned: Hybrid Sharepoint

1190. What is your working hypothesis, if you have one?

1191. What is your strategy for data collection?

1192. How much communication is socially oriented?

1193. Who is responsible for each action?

1194. What did you put in place to ensure success?

1195. How spontaneous are the communications?

1196. Were any strategies or activities unsuccessful?

1197. How do individuals resolve conflict?

1198. Did the team work well together?

1199. How much time is required for the task?

1200. What worked well/did not work well?

1201. How effective was the documentation that you received with the Hybrid Sharepoint project product/service?

1202. What are the external dependencies?

1203. How accurately and timely was the Risk

Management Log updated or reviewed?

1204. Were the aims and objectives achieved?

1205. Recommendation: what do you recommend should be done to ensure that others throughout your organization can benefit from what you have learned?

1206. Were the Hybrid Sharepoint project goals attained?

1207. What were the success factors?

Index

ability 33
abroad 131
accept 167
acceptable 189, 209, 233
acceptance 6, 142, 179, 217, 221, 248-249, 254
accepted 135, 147, 172, 179
accepting 206
access 2, 9-10, 24, 45, 50, 53, 55, 89, 92, 100, 103, 109, 179, 186, 207, 234
accessing 95, 112
accomplish 7, 90, 95, 190, 227
according 31, 33, 197, 244
account 11, 34, 88, 151, 181-182, 228
accounted 42, 172
accounting 188, 241, 252
accounts 99, 151
accuracy 37, 147, 236, 245
accurate 10, 36, 52, 209, 236
accurately 126, 258
achievable 190
achieve 7, 183, 185, 191, 204, 230, 243
achieved 19, 248, 259
achieving 133, 221
acquire 216
acquired 158
across 18, 53, 72-73, 88, 117-118
action 152, 168, 185, 198, 201, 209-210, 225, 258
actions 74, 151-152, 185, 190, 198, 203, 226
active 91, 101, 148, 205
actively 74, 193
activities 87, 90, 140, 155-157, 159, 161-162, 171-172, 175, 183, 198, 211, 258
activity 3-4, 28-29, 86, 108, 153, 155-157, 159, 161-163, 167, 170-171, 175, 188, 226
actual 28, 152, 188, 240-241, 247
actually 27, 99, 190, 230, 243
adapted 55
adaptive 232
addition 8, 189
additional 26, 35, 177, 226

additions   71
address   64, 110, 113, 185
addressed   66, 164, 194, 229, 249, 257
addressing   19, 33
adequate   145, 147-148, 154, 173, 199, 206, 211, 230
adequately   35, 172, 207
adjusted   222
adopters   234
adopting   88
adoption   44, 47, 85, 88, 92, 97-99, 106, 115, 118, 120, 245
adopts 109
advance   92, 229
advantage   184, 253
advantages   66, 106, 141
adverse   151
advice 245
affect 100, 106, 143, 146, 181, 197, 200, 213-214, 219-220, 229, 231
affected   131-132, 137, 192, 211
affecting   13
afford 86
affordable   110
against30, 201, 240, 249
agenda   126, 229, 244
agents 185
agility   21
agreed   41, 192
agreement   5, 139, 228-229
agreements   46, 109, 242
aligned   22
alignment   133
alleged   1
all-in   110
allocate   175, 240
allocated   151, 228, 241
allocation   228
allowed   86, 165
allowing   99
allows 10, 81
almost 242
already   51, 95, 110, 152, 183, 188, 211, 215, 256
altogether   201
always 10

Amazon	11
ambitious	230
Amongst	198
amount	20
amounts	50
analogous	167
analysis	3, 6, 12, 36-37, 39, 60-61, 63, 65, 131, 135, 138, 153, 165, 173, 178-179, 192, 202-203, 207, 218, 240-241
analytics	41
ANALYZE	2, 43, 64
analyzed	40-41, 59, 138, 154, 224
another	11, 44, 157, 200
anothers	231
answer	12-13, 17, 25, 36, 43, 58, 68, 77, 181
answered	24, 35, 42, 57, 67, 76, 123
answering	12, 246
anyone	35
anything	163, 183, 195, 222
appear	1
appetites	244
applicable	13, 48, 171, 221, 224, 245-246, 253
applied	70, 133, 158
appointed	27-28
approach	50, 92, 112, 147, 153, 175, 215, 231, 234, 238, 244-245
approached	85
approaches	98, 234
approval	229
approvals	79, 137, 140
approve	139
approved	21, 135, 143, 153, 174, 180, 210-211, 219-220
approving	143
architect	18, 92, 115, 120, 146
Architects	7
archive	44, 122
archives	254
archiving	117
argument	109
around	60, 63, 95, 98, 120, 231, 234, 241
articulate	231
ascertain	152
asking	1, 7, 96, 118, 180
aspect	194

aspects   208, 239
aspiration   230
assess 199
assessing   138
assessment   4-5, 9-10, 18, 134, 138, 140, 153, 190, 199, 205, 230, 232-233
assets 131, 250
assigned   28, 31, 128, 137, 145, 149, 151-152, 157, 226, 234
Assignment   4, 187-188
assist 9, 62, 177, 187
assistant   7
associated   64, 141-142, 201, 208, 224, 244
Assume   197, 233
Assumption   3, 147
assurance   137, 145, 173, 206, 221
assure 37, 223
attack 23
attainable   32, 190
attained   259
attempted   35
attendance   28
attendant   62
attended   28
attending   223
attention   13, 196
attitude   254
attitudes   215
attribute   191
attributes   3, 157, 217
audiences   105, 108, 212
audited   254
auditing   75, 94, 188, 224
Auditor 244
auditors   99, 245
audits 99, 223
Augmented   86
auspices   8
author 1
authority   138-139, 193
authorize   217
authorized   138, 152, 241, 254-255
Authorship   60
automated   138

automatic   254
automating   79, 119
available   22, 30, 35, 103-104, 107, 109, 113, 116, 156, 158, 162, 173, 175, 195, 202, 204, 222, 240
Average   13, 24, 35, 42, 57, 67, 76, 124, 221, 246
avoidance   195
awarded   252
awardee   208
backed   52
back-end   111
background   11, 31
backing   159
backup   44, 52-53, 65, 69, 75, 90, 102, 112, 122, 146
backups   77
backward   219
bandwidth   246
barrier 93
barriers 113, 120
Baseline   4, 42, 45, 179, 191
baselined   37, 205
baselines   180
bearers   245
become   71, 106, 121, 143, 221
becomes   222
becoming   23
before 10, 35, 161, 170, 173, 218
beginning   2, 16, 24, 35, 42, 57, 67, 76, 124
behavior   231, 238, 254
behaviors   189, 239
behaviours   211
behind 88, 97
belief   12, 17, 25, 36, 43, 58, 68, 77
believe 35, 62
beneficial   183
benefit 1, 21, 23, 61, 74, 98, 112, 123, 138, 167, 259
benefited   168
benefits   21, 44, 77, 82, 87, 102, 110, 112, 117, 148, 161, 253
better 7, 25, 73, 122, 156, 177, 204, 221-222, 226, 228, 230, 249
between   38, 54, 77, 81, 83, 85, 106, 118, 122, 127, 133, 143, 206, 209-210, 217, 238
biased 202, 252
biggest   100, 127, 183, 213

Blokdyk 8
Boolean 119
bothered 234
bottleneck 155
bought 11
boundaries 31, 117
bounds 31
bracketing 119
breach 54
Breakdown 3, 58, 149, 165
briefed 27
brings 33
broader 230
budget 58, 135, 155, 169, 171-172, 180, 213, 228, 246-247
Budgeted 151
budgets 151-152, 187-188, 240
building 69, 102, 128, 188, 242-243
burdensome 244
burn-in 249
business 1, 7, 11, 19, 21, 32, 44-45, 47-48, 50, 55, 69, 77-78, 80, 86, 91, 94, 98, 102, 104, 106, 109, 111, 117-118, 122, 136, 140-142, 152, 175, 179, 183, 212, 220, 241, 244-245, 248, 256
businesses 96
businesss 120
button 11
buy-in 249
buying 253
calculated 253
calendars 154
candidates 60
cannot 28, 161, 175
capability 41, 82, 117, 138, 147, 179
capable 7, 31
capacity 22, 69, 121
capital 41
capture 43, 71, 93, 255
captured 54, 56, 138, 154, 210
capturing 222
career 143, 190
carried 203
cash-drain 132
Cashflow 132
caused 1

causes 43, 51, 74, 133, 135, 152, 241
causing 147
celebrate 227
celebrated 233
center 47-48, 53, 95
centers 121
central 196, 222
certain 64, 235
Certified 137
certifier 61
chaired 8
challenge 7, 100, 123
challenges 47, 66, 89, 113, 159, 191
champion 31
chances 200
change 5, 17-19, 30, 83, 95, 99, 123, 130, 135, 139-140, 145, 150, 158, 161, 175, 184-185, 192, 211-212, 217-220, 237, 245, 254-255
changed 30, 111, 141, 167, 171, 175, 178, 211
changes 21, 38, 40, 62, 71, 113, 128, 138, 140, 146, 148, 151, 165, 168, 173-174, 180, 189, 192, 211, 217-219, 226, 241, 255
changing 108
channel 127
channels 202, 236
chargeable 188
charges 175
Charter 2, 28, 31, 128, 192, 205
charters 32
charts 40-41
checked 69-70, 75, 141
checklist 8
checklists 9
checks 31, 153, 252
choice 88, 92, 101
choose 12, 81, 83, 86, 96, 99, 107, 116, 245
choosing 86, 95, 118
chosen 128, 203, 236, 253
circumvent 20
claimed 1
claims 184
classified 151, 207
classify 52
clauses 252

clearly 12, 17, 25, 36, 43, 58, 68, 77, 138, 142, 190, 195, 206, 231
client   8, 11, 56, 87, 89, 136, 203, 248, 250
clients 72, 118
closed 75, 154, 219, 254
closely 11
Close-Out   6, 254, 256
Closing 6, 250
clouds 28, 37, 69, 73, 75, 77, 80-81, 88, 103, 117-118, 122
coaches   26, 31, 185-186
cognizant   233
coherent   191, 206
colleagues   169
collect 178, 185, 226
collected   25, 32, 36-37, 59
collection   37, 39, 186, 258
collective   253
combine   88
combined   55
coming   46, 99
comments   249
commitment   185
committed   34, 111, 174
committee   148, 174, 205, 217
common   43, 138, 172, 175, 208
community   83, 140, 169, 177-178, 197, 203
companies   1, 8, 221
company   7
comparable   135
compare   242
compared   201
comparing   135
comparison   12
compatible   219, 239
compelling   27, 109
competency   121
competitor   240
complain   183
complaint   224
complaints   184, 197, 224, 245
complete   1, 9, 12, 27, 157, 162, 169-170, 183, 191, 209, 228, 248, 255-256
completed   13, 29-30, 32, 34, 155, 161, 173, 205, 227, 254
completely   138

267

completing	110, 150
completion	29, 34, 61, 161, 188, 223, 227, 238, 242, 256
complex	7, 119, 171, 181, 242
complexity	108, 111, 173, 217
compliance	173, 224
compliant	85, 94, 121
complied	226
component	224
components	40-41, 153, 171, 195
compute	13
computer	147
computing	21, 33, 36, 38, 76, 80-81, 84, 92, 97, 102, 106, 111, 113, 115, 122
concept	186
concepts	181, 252
concerned	20, 107
concerns	19, 61, 110, 120, 194, 246
concise	139
concrete	231, 239
concurrent	18
condition	75, 134
conditions	75, 132, 135, 179, 226
conducted	65, 108, 138, 148, 173-174, 179, 244
confidence	196
confident	161
configure	111
confirm	13
conflict	131, 193, 229, 258
conflicts	172, 214, 227, 252
confront	211
connect	88, 105
connected	114
consensus	228, 256
consider	19-20, 61, 86, 89, 101, 121, 229
considered	20, 221
considers	181
consistent	49, 70, 152, 187, 224, 239, 241
constantly	193
constitute	230
Constraint	3, 147, 244
consultant	7
consulted	187, 194
consulting	244

consume 109
Contact 7
contain 22, 75, 231
contained 1
container 78
contains 9
content 26-27, 49, 60, 62, 75, 82, 98, 108, 116, 218, 221
contents 1-2, 9, 234
continual 11, 74, 76
continued 85
contract 6, 174, 176, 188, 216, 226, 240, 245, 252-255
contractor 6, 53, 146, 207, 240, 246
contracts 160, 247, 254
contribute 27, 131, 224, 257
control 2, 50, 53, 58, 68, 71-73, 132, 140, 145, 151-152, 154, 177, 206, 213, 217, 221, 245, 253
controlled 75, 187, 234, 256
controls 18, 22, 70, 161, 203, 245, 252
Conundrum 92
converge 239
convey 1, 137
conveyed 49
cooperate 178
Copyright 1
corporate 71, 111
correct 36, 68
corrective 74, 152, 168, 197, 225
correctly 70
correspond 9, 11
corrupt 44
corruption 252
counting 152
country 54
course 30, 242
covered 126
covering 9, 189
crashing 161
create 11, 20, 56, 99, 109-110, 140, 182, 217
created 130, 203
creates 70
creating 7, 105, 133, 147
creation 64, 195
creativity 60

credible 178
crisis 21
criteria 2, 5, 9, 11, 32, 62, 78, 125, 135, 142-143, 178, 207, 254
CRITERION 2, 17, 25, 36, 43, 58, 68, 77
critical 25-26, 48, 53, 72, 111, 154-155, 214, 222, 238, 250
criticized 81
crucial 52, 132
crystal 13
cultural 64
culture 116, 137, 184, 212
cumbersome 123
current 33, 36, 38, 80, 88, 141, 148, 153, 185, 189, 191, 198-199, 211, 213-214, 218, 250
currently 33, 60, 77, 91, 97, 100, 105, 120, 222, 240
custody 54
customer 11, 20, 25, 29, 31-32, 40, 50, 54, 56, 70, 72, 104, 112, 119, 129, 179, 195-196, 199, 202, 217, 249
customers 1, 22, 31-32, 34, 79, 81, 100, 104, 113-114, 118, 137, 141, 160, 181, 200-201, 203, 216, 240
cutbacks 82
cut-down 242
cycles 96
damage 1, 195
damaged 209
Dashboard 9
dashboards 71
database 53
databases 186
datasets 55
day-to-day 74
deadlines 160
dealing 113, 245
decide 46, 182
decided 227
decision 5, 175, 207, 221-222, 228
decisions 61, 64, 128, 175, 213, 221-222, 226, 228, 252, 256
dedicated 7, 111
deductions 252
deeper 13, 230
deeply 199
default 56, 114
defect 41, 225
defective 201, 244

defects 40, 127
defenders 85
define 2, 25, 33, 138, 183, 222, 238
defined 12-13, 17, 22, 25, 31, 34, 36, 40, 43, 58, 68, 77, 126, 138, 146-147, 149, 151, 153, 158, 167, 171, 190-191, 206, 251
defines 165
defining 7, 206
definite 75, 158
definition 148, 179, 201
degree 196, 230-233, 238-239
delays 170, 172
delegate 228
delegated 31
deletions 71
deliver 19, 22, 25, 44, 48, 78, 114, 175, 177, 228, 244
delivered 89, 166, 179, 236
delivery 41, 118, 159, 161, 201, 244, 254, 257
demand 202
demands 199, 239
department 7, 108, 215, 253
depend 48, 215
dependent 140
depends 84
deploy 72, 78, 93, 98
deployed 69, 78, 85, 88, 140
deployment 38, 63, 92, 121
Describe 47, 65, 128, 143, 246, 256
described 1, 141, 151, 195, 219, 253
describing 32, 168
deserving 215
design 1, 8, 11, 59-60, 63, 65, 88, 134, 202, 209, 236, 240
designated 191
designed 7, 11, 46, 62-63, 223
designer 20
designing 7
desired 26, 35, 165, 219, 243, 250
destroyed 49
detail 128, 138, 146, 149, 157
detailed 139, 148, 173
details 111
detect 75
detected 47
detection 82

determine	11-12, 70, 97, 156, 167-168, 178, 181-182, 207
determined	186, 200-201
determines	119
develop	22, 58, 65, 140, 149, 231
developed	8, 11, 30-32, 34, 59, 62-64, 72-73, 135, 145, 147, 153, 155, 192, 220, 224, 237, 242-243
developer	195
developing	66, 187, 207
develops	232
deviation	167
device	108, 224
devices	55, 122, 223
DevOps	21, 116
diagram	3, 135, 161
Diagrams	181
Dictionary	3, 151
differ	103
difference	54, 133-134, 145, 171, 209, 222
different	7, 27, 31, 34, 59, 132, 153, 190, 199, 210, 221, 253, 256
difficult	157
difficulty	213
direct	151-152, 188, 241
direction	30, 99, 135
directions	203
directly	1, 257
directory	5, 43, 91, 101, 226
Disagree	12, 17, 25, 36, 43, 58, 68, 77
disaster	38, 51-52, 90, 118, 172
disasters	85
discovered	64
discovery	18
discus	253
display	41, 160
displayed	25, 37, 40, 156
disputes	254
disregard	167
disrupt	82
disruption	44
distressed	223
distribute	227
Divided	24, 31, 35, 42, 57, 67, 76, 123
document	11, 27, 73, 126, 128, 140, 147, 221, 226, 250

documented 33, 61, 69-71, 73, 126, 141, 145, 147-148, 174, 180, 182, 189-190, 209, 218, 248, 251
documents 7, 41, 61, 64, 183, 210
dollars 152
domain 113
downsides 87
drafted 46
drawings 224
drivers 44-47, 55
drives 43, 47
driving 85, 95, 97, 123
duplicate 182
Duration 3-4, 134, 149, 162, 167, 169
durations 28
during 30, 66, 157, 163, 173, 187, 200-201, 222-223, 232, 257
duties 217
dynamics 33
earned 6, 187, 242-243
economic 200, 203
economies 131
economy 131, 213
eDiscovery 222
edition 9
editorial 1
educate 256
education 71
effect 134, 200
effective 20, 84-85, 105-106, 152, 222-225, 233, 244-245, 253, 258
effects 132, 159, 198
efficiency 108
efficient 134, 215, 253
effort 38, 103, 151, 153, 224
efforts 35, 83, 173
elasticity 30, 81
Electrical 73
electronic 1, 61
element 151, 188, 240
elements 11-12, 128, 146, 152, 188, 191, 205-206, 253
eliminate 203
eliminated 82
e-mail 114, 117
embark 79

embarking 27
embrace 212
emergency 244
emerging 70
empirical 244
employed 167, 205
employee 31, 247
employees 18, 224, 233
employers 130
empower 7
enable 109
enabled 118
enablement 87
encourage 60, 230
encourages 182
encrypted 45, 52, 56
encryption 89
endpoints 48
end-to-end 46
endure 176
engage 63, 229-230, 238
engaged 236
engagement 130, 193
Engineers 73
enhance 245
enough 7, 21, 69, 140, 143, 213
ensure 28, 30, 54, 62-63, 85, 89, 97-100, 117, 122, 147, 154, 176, 182, 185, 189, 227, 230, 236, 252-253, 258-259
ensured 252
ensures 70
ensuring 10, 242-243
entering 245
enterprise 41, 54, 79, 82-83, 88-89, 91, 98, 100, 102, 107, 216
entire 114
entitled 56
entity 1, 232
entrusted 54
equally 48
equipment 26, 214
equipped 30, 79
equitably 31, 230
equivalent 151
errors 19, 127

especially 211
essence 129, 137
essential 230
establish 58, 177, 195
estimate 135, 167, 176, 196, 208, 211, 248
estimated 29, 34, 174, 177-178, 196, 246-247, 252
Estimates 3-4, 33, 135, 138, 148, 167, 175
Estimating 4, 138, 169, 177
estimation 205
estimator 176
ethical 249
evaluate 62, 66, 173, 241, 252
evaluated 65
evaluating 62
evaluation 135, 183, 207-208, 232
events 167, 200
everyone 30-31, 88
everything 80, 100, 221
evidence 13, 197, 207, 215
evolution 36
evolve 74
exactly 116, 183
example 2, 9, 14, 70, 73, 135, 147
examples 7, 9, 11, 237
exceed 149, 162
excellence 7
exception 233
excess 188, 240
exchange 238
execute 213, 249
executed 37, 219
Executing 5, 213
execution 226
executive 7, 153
executives 99
Exercise 162
exercises 230
existing 11-12, 45-46, 82, 89, 91, 93, 101, 108, 123, 135, 146
expect 51, 79-80, 83, 92, 107, 118, 121, 139, 169, 201
expected 21, 28, 84, 87, 135, 221, 224, 236, 253, 257
expense 188, 240
expenses 40-41, 228, 240
experience 40, 99, 104, 169, 189, 196, 247

experts 26
explained   11
explore   238
explored   181
expose 54, 56
exposed   50
expressed   136, 244
extent 12, 17, 20, 23, 32, 65, 133-134, 224, 232
external   27, 35, 99, 105, 131, 152, 154, 199, 224, 258
extreme   230
facilitate   12, 65, 71, 238
facing 20, 197
fact-based   238
factors 95, 177, 259
failover 26
failures 122
fairly   31
falling   97
familiar 9
fashion 1, 28
favorable   152
feasible   154, 177, 195
feature 10
features   62, 135, 181, 195
federation   116, 123
feedback   2, 11, 29, 32, 228
figure   41
finalized   14
financial   44, 131, 159, 244
fingertips   10
finish   156, 158-159, 161, 242-243
flavor   109
flexible 17
focused   17
focuses   127
folders 114
follow   11, 43, 73, 162, 229, 249
followed   33, 152, 173, 192, 207
following   9, 12, 185
follow-on   250
forces 85, 184
forecast   243
foresee   159

forget 10
formal 6, 109, 137, 139, 148, 191, 224, 238-239, 248-249
formally   138, 172
format 11, 27, 45, 50, 146, 218, 226
formats   198
formatting   61
formed 31, 34, 232
formula   13
Formulate   25
forward   99, 107
fragmented   49
framework   133
frequency   75, 186
frequent   145, 173, 191, 205
frequently   131, 228, 238
friends 230
full-scale   59
fulltime 111, 174
function   113, 145, 173, 175, 217, 256
functional   152
functions   97, 103, 141, 165
funded 153, 250
funding   64, 140, 148
future 7, 22, 36, 72-73, 85, 88, 93-94, 110, 133, 135, 191, 198-199, 232
gained 69, 74
Gather 12, 36
General   244, 248
generally   215
generate   60-61
generated   61
generation   9
geographic   131
Gerardus   8
getting 123, 194
Google   22, 61, 109
govern 111, 238
governance   53, 70, 119, 133, 174, 182, 190
governing   193
government   105
graded   197, 217
granted   179
graphs 9, 40

greater 133, 135
ground 38, 44
groups 106, 119, 137, 148, 187, 192, 211-212, 216, 238
growth 51, 123
guaranteed 29
guidance 1
guidelines 118, 136, 252
guiding 207, 223
handle 163, 203, 226
handled 45, 208, 229
handling 223-224
happen 22, 159, 197
happened 126
happening 61
happens 7, 11, 22, 47, 61, 79, 175, 177, 197, 203, 224, 254
hardened 106
hardly 242
hardware 26, 147
harness 43
having 228, 240
hazards 203
hazmat 245
health 39, 137, 209, 223
healthy 182
heavily 51
helpful 39, 187
helping 7, 133, 138
higher 109
highest 18, 104
high-level 29-30, 142
highlight 189
hiring 71
historical 177
history 155
hitting 242
holding 114
hosted 32, 54, 56
hosting 101
housing 53
humans 7

Hybrid 1-6, 9-15, 17-39, 41-42, 46, 50, 54-57, 59-62, 64-67, 69, 71-74, 76, 78-79, 81-90, 92-94, 96-107, 109-113, 115-118, 120-131, 133-141, 143, 145-159, 161-163, 165, 167-183, 185, 187, 189-193, 195, 197, 199-201, 203, 205-209, 211, 213-219, 221, 223, 226-228, 230, 232, 234, 236-242, 244, 246, 248-254, 256-259
hybrids 111
hypotheses   43
hypothesis   258
identified   1, 20, 23, 25, 31, 37, 40-41, 145, 147, 151-152, 154, 167, 174, 179-180, 187, 189, 203, 206, 208, 224, 229, 237, 251, 253
identify 12, 20, 131, 152, 168, 178, 191, 193, 211, 223, 240
identity 103
imbedded   74
immediate   38, 132
impact 4, 29, 31, 36, 38, 40-41, 65, 133, 141, 168, 174, 179-180, 197-199, 201, 212-213, 219, 226, 234, 237, 241, 250
impacted   41, 148, 211-212
impacts   131, 147-148, 169, 210
implement   29, 68, 84
importance   239
important   20, 54, 59, 62, 75, 78, 86-87, 89-90, 95, 102, 127-128, 165, 181, 183-184, 193, 231
improve   2, 11-12, 44, 55, 58, 66, 127-128, 226, 256-257
improved   60, 63, 71, 133, 251
improving   215
inaccurate   140
inbound   26
incentives   71
incident   85, 118, 197, 222
include   49, 151, 155, 192, 209, 218, 252
included   2, 9, 30, 153, 178, 183, 217, 240, 246, 254
includes   10, 39
including   26, 28, 30, 58, 224
inclusion   224
incomplete   140
increase   17, 92, 181, 199
increased   190, 244
incurrence   188, 240
indemnity   105
in-depth   9, 12
indicate   41, 75, 224
indicated   74
indicators   195

indirect 65, 151, 175, 188, 240
indirectly 1
individual 1, 155, 228, 231, 238, 246, 256
inducting 223
industries 81
industry 245
influence 130, 133, 138, 221-222, 232, 256
influences 229, 234
inform 231
informal 239
ingrained 72
inherited 84
inhibit 64
in-house 96, 128
initial 55, 153, 181
initiate 152
initiated 177, 220
Initiating 2, 126
initiative 12, 47, 185, 194, 211
innovate 58, 96
innovation 132, 182
innovative 177, 236
inputs 32, 34, 75, 126, 128, 167-168
insider 81
insights 9, 38
inspection 197
installed 114
Institute 73
instructed 140
integrate 59, 94-95, 101
integrated 115
integrity 19, 38, 219
intend 62
intended 1, 62, 198
INTENT 17, 25, 36, 43, 58, 68, 77
intention 1
intentions 224
interest 194, 216, 252
interests 20
interface 46, 102
interfaces 20
internal 1, 35, 55, 79, 102, 197, 245, 253
interpret 12-13

intervals 154
intranet 108
introduce 198-199
introduced 233
invaluable 2, 11
inventory 18
invest 24
invested 83, 95
investment 20, 185
involved 22, 64, 139, 148, 153, 190, 193, 201, 214-215, 233, 236, 253, 255-256
isolate 152
issuance 252
issued 252
issues 64, 126, 137-138, 146, 163, 172, 209-210, 214, 226, 229
itself 1, 19
Jabber 22
journey 79, 119
judgment 1
justify 197
keywords 70
knock-on 198
Knowing 137
knowledge 11, 35, 69, 71, 74, 189, 191, 211-212, 229, 255
kubernetes 48
languages 114
larger 17
latency 18, 80
latest 9
leader 31, 229
leaders 30-31, 118, 182, 231, 234
leadership 33, 145, 228
learned 6, 71, 173, 186, 248, 256, 258-259
learning 49, 74, 182, 222, 225, 232
legacy 28, 69
lesson 256
lessons 6, 59, 71, 173, 186, 248, 256, 258
levels 18, 73, 107, 117, 131, 138, 149, 154, 185, 203
leverage 29, 71, 169, 178
leveraged 35, 115
liability 1
licensed 1, 89
licenses 86, 89, 109-110

licensing   115
lifecycle   116, 199
Lifetime   10
likelihood   133, 197-198, 200, 209
likely   87, 179, 197, 199-200
limited 11, 28
lineage   50
Linked 26, 221
listed   1, 172
loaded 207
located   43, 51, 112
location   40-41, 50, 81, 102-103, 112, 119, 222
locations   54
logged 218
logical 161, 163
logically   153
logins   18
longer 24
long-term   73
looking 64, 94, 117
lowest 151, 162
machine   49
machines   69, 89
maintain   68, 182
maintained   187, 224
majority   228
makers 175
making   228
manage   63, 73, 80, 93, 111, 118, 120, 143, 163, 173, 175, 180, 191, 227, 234
manageable 32, 153
managed   7, 83, 86, 115, 168, 205, 210, 218, 248, 253
management 1, 3-5, 9, 11-12, 17-18, 20-21, 26, 28, 31, 47, 49, 51, 54, 58-59, 62, 64, 70, 82, 96-97, 101, 103, 105, 126, 132-133, 135-139, 145, 147-148, 151, 153-154, 158, 166-167, 169, 171, 173-175, 179-181, 185, 191-193, 195, 197-198, 200-201, 205-207, 209, 211, 213-216, 218, 224, 229, 236, 242, 244, 248, 250-251, 255-256, 259
manager   7, 12, 22, 29-30, 128, 135, 137, 145, 154, 167, 215, 248
managers   2, 80, 125, 152, 187
manages   70, 119, 128, 247
managing   2, 71, 98, 125-126, 130
mandatory   219

manner 152, 175, 187, 213, 241, 249, 253
mapped 34
margin 153
market 118, 196, 213, 240, 242
marketable 196
marketer 7
Master 171
material 128, 151, 159, 183-184, 187, 207, 240, 245
materials 1, 229
matrices 143
Matrix 3-4, 131, 143-144, 187, 201
matter 26, 88, 91
matters 221
mature 86, 140
maximize 223
maximum 102
meaning 158
meaningful 195, 231
measurable 29, 32, 127, 152
measure 2, 12, 19, 27, 29, 36-37, 39-40, 58, 177-178, 180, 183-184, 186, 213, 241
measured 40, 75, 151, 183, 230, 239, 244
measures 37, 41, 75, 197, 214, 218, 236, 239
measuring 151
mechanical 1
mechanism 93, 257
mechanisms 134, 186, 252
medium 242
meeting 28, 70, 87, 126, 189, 193, 216, 221, 227-229
meetings 28-29, 31, 126, 175, 187, 228
Member 5, 33, 165, 193, 215, 228, 232
members 26-28, 31, 33, 111, 139, 146, 153, 174, 187, 193, 207, 217, 227-232, 235, 238-239, 244
membership 230
memorable 231
messages 193, 257
metadata 70
method 135, 145, 170, 181, 183, 193-194, 217, 228
methods 29, 178, 182, 202, 205
metrics 4, 41, 71, 97, 112, 129, 138, 140, 173, 180, 183-184, 191, 195
Microsoft 22, 46, 54, 60, 62, 64, 102, 110
migrating 110

migration 20, 90, 116
migrations 87
milestone 3, 159-161, 205
milestones 28, 130, 158
minimize 53, 88, 133, 250
minimum 246
minority 20
minutes 28, 227-228
missing 81, 157, 179
mission 53, 111
Mitigate 133
mitigated 59, 251
mitigating 206
mitigation 135, 199
mix-ups 223
Modeling 185
models 38, 41, 49, 132
Modern 120
modernize 107
modified 23, 60, 101
modifier 183
moments 52
monetary 21
monitor 62, 69, 73-74, 178, 237
monitored 72, 137, 155, 168-169
monitoring 5, 68, 70-71, 74, 146, 152, 163, 187, 218, 236
monoliths 108
months 79
motion 52, 56
motivate 238
motivated 191
moving 55, 63, 66, 82, 100-101
multiple 80, 91, 205, 232
multitier 93
mutilated 252
mutual 133
naming 43
narrow 51
national 131, 203
native 84, 93
nearest 13
necessary 47, 59, 82, 137, 178, 187, 199, 219, 236, 252-253

needed 18, 24, 34, 68, 73, 170, 175, 185, 191, 207, 253, 257
negative 212
negatively 213-214
neither 1
nesting 119
network 3, 18, 34, 64-65, 68, 87, 97-98, 102, 106, 110, 118-119, 161
networking 66
networks 66
Neutral 12, 17, 25, 36, 43, 58, 68, 77
non-hybrid 87, 89, 140
non-IT 99
normal 72
Notice 1
noticing 222
notified 195, 212, 254
number 24, 35, 42, 57, 67, 76, 88, 102, 123, 157, 182, 199, 260
numerous 254-255
objective 7, 122, 129, 132, 175, 196, 221, 240
objectives 19-20, 22, 25-26, 87, 126, 135, 148, 174, 191, 198, 204, 216, 227, 233, 252, 257, 259
observe 189
observed 64
obstacles 20, 159, 177
obtain 78, 117, 167
obtained 32, 137
obvious 79
obviously 13
occurred 181
occurrence 195
occurring 66, 197, 202
occurs 21, 201, 225, 237, 250
offered 102
offeror 207
offers 208
office 27, 61, 126, 154, 216, 245, 254
officer 208
officers 244
officials 254
offline 109
onboarding 191

OneDrive   46, 54
one-time   7
ongoing   36, 64, 75, 155, 169
online 11, 32, 86, 105, 107, 123
onpremise   81
on-premise   41, 90, 100, 111, 115
on-site 226
operate   203
operating   5, 38, 40-41, 70, 228-229
operation   75, 179, 236
operations   12, 36, 61, 68, 71-72, 83, 108, 119, 179, 223
operators   73, 119, 183
opponents   132, 193
opposed   193
optimal   61, 63, 65, 246
optimized   63
optimiztic   167
option 116, 232, 245
options 22, 71, 91, 105, 109
orderly 223
orders 175, 252
organized   232
orient 70
oriented   258
origin 142
original 172, 205, 221
originally   153
originate   194
others 177-178, 180-181, 184, 189, 193-194, 196, 221, 238, 256, 259
otherwise   1, 64
outbound   26
outcome   13, 165, 226
outcomes   63, 177, 198, 225, 243, 250, 256
output 29, 39, 75
outputs   32, 75, 163, 167
outside 60, 62, 175, 229, 253
Outsource   254
outsourced   97
overall 12-13, 22, 127, 172, 181, 198, 221, 246
overcome   88, 177
overhead   151-152, 188, 240-241
overheads   206

overlooked 69, 250
overruns 40
oversight 146, 148, 154, 205, 233
overtime 163
owners 50, 149
ownership 44, 47, 69, 133
package 56, 122, 151
packages 152
packaging 245
parallel 161
parameters 72, 111
particular 39
Parties 255
partner 105, 119
partners 22, 34, 160, 256
patterns 22, 88
payment 173, 254
payroll 252
pending 219
people 7, 99, 131, 147, 168, 183, 186-188, 191, 199, 211, 213, 215, 242
perceived 201
percentage 49, 143, 184
perform 28, 31, 33, 85, 99, 140, 153, 165, 217, 230, 249
performed 77, 137, 143, 151-152, 155, 197, 226, 240
performing 84, 119, 126, 187, 233
perhaps 242
period 187, 240
periodic 97
permission 1
person 1, 160, 176
personally 143
personnel 21, 96, 161, 173, 185, 224
phases 158, 257
physically 44
picked 96
placed 95
placements 225
places 176
planned 37, 163, 169, 197-198, 206, 244, 256
planning 3, 9, 133, 148, 152, 155, 162-163, 216, 250
platform 20, 39, 96, 110, 112
platforms 79, 86, 91, 120

pocket 169
pockets   169
points 24, 35, 42, 57, 67, 76, 80, 100, 123, 186
policies   101, 119, 136, 211, 244
policy 121, 133, 164, 174, 182, 198, 224
political   64, 132, 199
popularity   38
portable   97, 122
portal 91, 101
portfolio   66
portion 171
position   189, 245
positioned   93, 177-178
positions   245
positive   135, 148
possess 230
possible   51, 60-61, 68, 99, 112, 187
possibly   201
post-test   232
potential   20, 59, 62, 66, 131, 141, 168, 204, 209, 232, 236, 241
powershell   119
practical   58, 68, 215-216
practice   123, 252
practices   1, 11, 22, 71, 237, 245
precaution   1
precede   161
precise 108
precludes   208
prediction   157
predictive   165
preferred   83, 257
pre-filled   9
premise   32, 51, 120
premises   105
prepare   123, 167, 185, 190
prepared   87
preparing   256
present   36, 73, 192, 205, 238, 253
presented   226
presenting   228
preserve   28
pressing   126

288

pressures   160
prevent   18-19, 23, 148, 223
prevented   223
previous   35, 159, 171, 247, 250
previously   138, 195, 219
pricing 207
primary   46-47, 90, 108, 139, 188
principles   88, 133, 136, 207, 233, 252
printing   8
prioritize   116
priority 239
privacy   135, 183
private 37, 39, 48, 52, 54, 60, 62, 64, 78, 83, 88, 92, 103, 105, 107, 110, 112, 116-117, 121
problem   17, 21-22, 25, 28, 32, 35, 132, 168, 215, 222, 238, 242
problems   19-22, 66, 74, 133, 141, 185, 208, 237
procedure   181, 223, 225, 245, 253
procedures   11, 69-71, 73, 94, 101, 137, 151-152, 164, 167-168, 171, 174, 181-182, 185-186, 206-207, 211, 221, 229, 244
proceeding   170
process   1-7, 11, 21, 27, 29-30, 32-34, 37-41, 47-48, 50, 52, 56, 60, 62-64, 69-76, 126, 128, 133, 140-143, 145, 148, 163, 167, 170, 173, 176, 181, 185-186, 191, 199, 201, 209, 213, 221, 226, 228, 231-232, 236, 242-243, 247-248, 250, 253, 257
processes   34, 44, 47, 55, 71, 126, 153, 185, 198, 211, 220, 229, 236, 251
processing   49, 55-56
procure   86
produce   126, 163, 175, 216, 236
producing   143
product   1, 11, 78, 140, 146, 179, 181, 196, 201, 203, 209, 215-216, 219, 226, 243-244, 248, 250, 258
production   79, 131, 229
productive   187
products   1, 58, 64, 109, 143, 214, 216, 219, 239, 244
profile 198
profit   122
program   21, 133, 189, 195, 198, 232, 236
programs   215, 244
progress   27, 178, 213, 237

project 2-7, 9, 23, 34, 55, 73, 84, 96, 103, 125-131, 133-140, 143, 145-150, 152-159, 161-162, 165, 167-178, 180-182, 187, 189-192, 195, 197, 199-201, 205-206, 208-209, 213-216, 218-219, 226-227, 236-239, 242, 246, 248-251, 253-254, 256-259
projected   78, 241
projects   2, 125-126, 131, 143, 172, 176, 201, 215-216, 227-228, 242, 257
promised   114
promotion   190
promptly   231
proofing   64
proper 151, 252
properly   11, 30, 106, 151
properties   97
proponents   193
proposal   159, 207-208, 250
proposals   167, 208
propose   40, 96, 123
proposed   62-63, 113, 120, 135, 138-139, 168, 207, 209, 246
protect   28, 44, 48, 56, 111, 116, 135
protected   48-49, 104, 109
protection   45, 49, 52, 109
protects   47
protocols   103, 209
provide   18, 21, 28, 40, 95, 109, 127, 130, 139, 141, 151, 154, 168, 177, 181, 183, 187-188, 213, 238
provided   8, 13, 50, 70, 92, 98, 105, 137, 147, 154, 173, 191, 207
provider   32, 44, 47-48, 50, 54, 56, 63, 70, 80, 85, 94, 99, 101, 106, 112, 114
providers   78, 89, 94, 106, 109, 113, 205
provides   141, 160
providing   26, 84, 104, 128, 130, 146, 171, 179
provision   221
proxies 90
public 37, 48, 50, 52, 54, 56, 60, 62, 64-65, 75, 77-78, 80, 82-83, 85, 90, 93, 95, 102-103, 105, 109, 114-115, 117, 121
published   211
publisher   1
publishing   62
punishment   115
purchase   9, 11, 214, 252-253
purchased   11, 209

purchases   110, 209
purpose   2, 11, 126, 129, 131, 177, 179, 188, 221, 229-231, 238
pursue 110
putting 55, 112
qualified   31, 145, 154
qualifiers   119
qualifying   171
quality 1, 4-5, 11, 39, 72, 134, 137, 145, 172-173, 179, 181-185, 191, 206, 221, 223-226
quantity   207
question   12-13, 17, 25, 36, 43, 58, 68, 77
questions   7, 9, 12, 89, 101, 169, 193, 208, 235
quickly 12, 101
raising   134
ranking 202
rather   110
rating   131, 217
ratings 207
rational   241
reader 137
readings   69
realised   209
realism 207
realistic   121, 135, 172, 232
reality   86, 153
realized   248
really   7, 22, 53, 88, 93, 109, 187
reason 51, 131
reasonable   135, 153, 175
reasons   27, 114, 152, 173, 184
re-assign   157
receipt 223
receive   9-10, 29, 193, 227
received   27, 174, 199, 224, 258
recently   11
recipient   24, 254
recognize   2, 17, 20-22
recognized   18-21, 23, 233, 244
recognizes   22
recommend   194, 259
record 185
recorded   154, 182, 218

recording 1
records 75, 187-188, 209, 254
recover 46
recovery 38, 51-52, 90, 118, 122, 148, 171
recurrence 204
re-define 230
reduce 40, 96, 134, 151, 198, 209-210
reduced 79
reducing 70
references 260
reflect 209, 256
reflected 238
refresh 49
refuses 203
regarding 45, 207, 215
Register 2, 4, 130, 197
registry 63
regular 21, 27, 31, 145, 246
regularly 27-28, 126, 175
regulated 51, 81
regulation 232
regulatory 26, 30, 102, 226
reject 212
relate 89, 214, 220
related 61, 73, 152, 179, 242, 257
relating 179
relation 112, 225
relative 239
release 140, 173, 257
releases 246
relevant 11, 32, 112, 179, 189, 191, 212, 226
reliable 30, 204
reliably 230
remaining 177
remedies 38
remember 170
remove 24, 64, 108, 203
rephrased 11
replace 94, 99, 250
replaced 134
replicate 182
report 5-6, 69, 160, 197, 207, 215, 224, 227, 238, 246, 256
reported 187, 234, 243

reporting 37, 73, 152, 198, 239, 245
reports 97, 130, 174, 191, 195
represent 219
reproduced 1
reputation 80
request 5, 91, 94, 96, 192, 208, 217-220
requested 1, 217, 219
requests 82, 102, 113, 218
require 30, 52-53, 164, 171, 195, 211, 232
required 27, 29, 31, 33, 73, 126-127, 157-158, 162, 170, 173, 186, 189, 191, 209, 211, 256, 258
requires 207
requiring 130, 255
research 160, 229, 232
reserved 1
reside 176
resides 44
resilience 28
resolution 152, 193
resolve 157, 227, 229, 258
resource 3-4, 148, 154, 157, 163, 165-166, 188, 191, 209, 213, 216, 228
resources 2, 9, 30, 35, 58, 103, 128, 131, 141, 145, 147, 154, 157-158, 161-162, 165, 169, 173, 178, 188, 206, 209, 226, 236-238
respect 1, 86
respective 133
respond 85, 101, 188
responded 13
response 21, 69, 74-75, 82, 85, 118, 246
responses 224
responsive 169, 177
restore 44
result 117, 146, 177, 180, 219, 231, 254
resulted 70
resulting 44, 135
results 9, 17, 25, 28, 58, 70, 133, 137, 175-177, 186, 236, 240, 248
retain 46, 51, 77
retained 18, 252
retention 53
return 161, 185
returns 184
revenue 244
reverse 90

review 11-12, 161, 172, 187, 197, 209, 229
reviewed   30, 46, 127, 153, 172, 182, 259
reviews 11, 137, 148, 174, 196, 240
revised 70, 203
revisions   255
revisit   222
Reward   115, 215
rewarded   18
rewards   71, 107
rights   1, 99, 113
roadmap   41, 58, 66
robust   252
routine 72
running   39, 93, 103, 119-120
rushing 193
safely   118, 203
safety   209, 229, 244
samples   182
sampling   182
satisfied   176, 248-250
satisfies 242
satisfy   18
savings 33, 81
scalable   90
scenario   168
schedule   3-4, 33, 58, 133, 135, 142, 152-154, 161, 171-172, 174, 179-180, 187, 192, 195, 197, 214, 218, 220, 240-241, 246, 251
scheduled   139, 175, 252
schedules   146, 153
scheduling   92, 239
scheme   76
Science   170
scientific   170
Scorecard   2, 13-15
scorecards   71
Scores 15
scoring 11
screening   135
script   49
seamless   87
search 54, 70, 119
searches   119
searching   53

seasonal 26
second 13
section 13, 24, 35, 42, 57, 67, 76, 123-124
sector 78, 242
secure 52-53, 56, 73, 86, 89, 93, 103
secured 55, 106
securely 99, 253
security 26, 28, 53, 55-56, 66, 72, 88, 93, 95, 97, 100, 107, 111, 117, 130, 147, 196, 219, 223, 257
segmented 31
segments 34
select 78
selected 62, 65, 135, 177-178, 201, 208
selecting 135, 214
Selection 5, 207, 230
selects 232
seller 176
sellers 1, 167
selling 221
senior 182
sensitive 54, 80, 88
separate 92, 110
separated 151
sequence 155, 161
series 12
serious 140
server 60, 87, 100, 120
servers 23, 61, 81, 113
service 1-2, 7-8, 11, 18, 47, 83-85, 87, 91, 94, 96, 98, 101, 103-104, 106-107, 113-114, 116, 118, 146, 179, 181, 198, 215-216, 258
services 1, 8, 21, 30, 48, 60-61, 72, 82-83, 86, 89, 91-92, 94-96, 100, 103, 105, 107, 113, 115-116, 118, 121, 123, 228, 236, 240, 246-247, 249, 253-254
serving 93
session 155
several 8, 55
shared 43, 69, 92, 141, 177, 221, 228, 240
Sharepoint 1-6, 9-15, 17-22, 24-35, 41-42, 57, 60, 62-65, 67, 72-76, 82, 86, 88-89, 91-92, 96, 101-102, 105, 107-109, 115, 119-120, 124-131, 133-141, 143, 145-159, 161-163, 165, 167-183, 185, 187, 189-193, 195, 197, 199-201, 203, 205-209, 211, 213-219, 221, 223, 226-228, 230, 232, 234, 236-242, 244, 246, 248-254, 256-259
sharing 46, 71

short-term 64, 230
should 7, 24, 27, 30, 44-45, 55, 60, 63, 66, 73, 82-83, 85-86, 95, 97, 107, 113, 116, 119, 121, 123, 130, 133-134, 136, 139, 155, 160, 165-167, 169, 179, 183, 185, 189-190, 195-196, 198-201, 204, 207-208, 226-227, 237, 250, 256, 259
-should 180
signatures 164
signed 146
signers 254
sign-in 104
sign-on 83, 91, 101
similar 34-35, 155, 235
simple 242
simply 9, 11, 113, 244
simulator 230
single 83, 91, 100-101, 104, 110, 175, 229, 232
single-use 7
situation 18, 36, 175, 197, 242
situations 230
skilling 83
skills 18, 22, 60, 126, 173, 179, 187, 189, 191, 209, 211, 213, 231, 233, 253
smaller 133
social 86, 113, 203
socially 258
software 56, 134, 138-139, 142, 167, 172, 200, 224, 246
solicit 29, 228
soliciting 228
solution 37, 41, 47-48, 58-66, 68, 74, 146, 203, 246
solutions 46, 55, 59-62, 64-66
solved 23
solving 238
Someone 7
something 136, 180, 210
sought 131
source 5, 176, 204, 207, 224
sources 64, 142, 167
special 70, 207
specific 9, 19, 29, 32, 99, 105, 108, 140, 147, 157, 159, 164, 175, 181, 189, 208, 212, 216, 220
specified 26, 152
specify 239
sponsor 20, 135, 249

sponsored 31
sponsors 22, 175, 185
sprawl 71
stability 37, 183
stable 78, 106, 140
staffed 35
staffing 71, 136, 148
stages 223
standard 7, 71, 163, 167, 246
standards 1, 11-12, 70, 72-73, 75-76, 147, 174, 183, 185, 220, 240, 244
started 9, 161
starting 12
starts 134
start-up 132
stated 110, 142, 152, 183, 188, 211, 256
Statement 3, 12, 129, 145, 147, 205
statements 13, 24, 28, 32, 35, 42, 57, 67, 76, 123
status 5-6, 137, 152-153, 174, 191, 195, 215, 218, 227, 242, 246
statute 232
statutory 173, 226
steady 81
steering 148, 153, 174, 205
stopped 47
storage 23, 45-47, 54, 63, 72, 75, 78, 81-82, 85, 98, 119-120, 122, 186, 218, 223, 238
storages 75
stored 41, 44-46, 54-55, 85, 89, 139, 253
storing 48
strategic 98
strategies 146, 199, 211, 221-222, 258
strategy 22, 27, 53, 59, 65-66, 82, 84, 95, 98-99, 104, 107, 109, 118, 120, 147, 176, 191, 195, 198, 206, 221, 252-253, 257-258
strengths 137, 228
strong 189
Strongly 12, 17, 25, 36, 43, 58, 68, 77
structure 3, 43, 58, 96, 149, 165, 211-212
structured 153
structures 19, 238-239
subfactor 208
subHybrid 199-200
subject 9-10, 26
submit 11

submitted 11, 219-220
success 19, 24, 27, 127, 147, 154, 213, 215, 222, 230, 250, 257-259
successful 62, 75, 133-134, 165, 195, 216, 237
sufficient 75, 134
suggested 74, 219
suitable 40, 60, 69, 94, 117, 195
suited 80, 122
supervisor 189, 228
supplier 87, 223
suppliers 32, 224-225, 252
supply 211
support 7, 21, 46-48, 59, 74-75, 78, 96, 103, 108, 110-111, 116, 122, 131, 138, 141, 164, 212, 222, 224, 228, 246, 252
supported 34, 90, 101, 114, 199
supporters 131
supporting 108, 137
supports 81, 228
surface 74
SUSTAIN 2, 77
sustained 176, 237
sustaining 73
switch 92
symptom 17
system 11-12, 20, 38, 46, 49, 61, 69, 78, 85, 87-88, 91, 100-101, 103, 110, 113, 120, 128, 131, 139, 141-142, 147, 151, 188, 209, 219, 222-225, 240-243
systematic 187
systems 18, 39, 53, 62, 71, 79, 84, 88, 120, 145, 173, 242, 248, 253
tables 181
tactics 222
taking 126, 181, 215, 228
talking 7
tangle 187
target 34, 37, 55, 108, 184, 205, 212
targeted 105
targets 127, 242
tasked 69
technical 47, 64, 76, 131, 141, 159, 207
techniques 167, 200
technology 46, 62-64, 72, 86, 95, 110, 114, 132, 141, 195, 200, 229

template   171
templates   7, 9
tenant 92
tenants   92
testable   141
test-cycle   186
tested 61, 65
testing 62, 65, 101, 141, 195, 202, 232, 245
thankful   8
thematic   131
themes 231
therefore   204
things   123, 127, 175, 201, 205, 236
thinking   60-61, 112
thorough   179
thought   234
threat 81
through   21, 199, 222-223
throughout   1, 259
throughput   26
time-bound   32
timeframe   158, 178
timeline   220
timely   28, 175, 213, 223, 226, 228, 241, 258
Timescales   160
timing 232
together   77, 229, 258
tolerable   203
tolerated   156, 244
tomorrow   126
topologies   123
topology   97
touched   142
toward 70, 87, 215
towards   114, 131
traced 179
tracking   27, 145-146, 148
trademark   1
trademarks   1
Tradeoff   207, 244
trade-offs   206
trained 30, 33-34, 181, 207
training   70-72, 189, 199, 209, 211, 213, 215, 229, 232

Transfer 13, 24, 35, 42, 57, 67, 69, 71, 76, 86, 124, 246
transform 97
transition 50, 83
translated 29
transport 245
treasurer 244
trends 135, 200, 203
trying 7, 21, 90, 128, 139, 204
turnaround 158
turnkey 122
two-page 168
typical 116, 119, 213, 234
typically 89
underlying 63
understand 25, 189, 231
understood 200-201, 231
unified 27, 112
unique 28
Unless 7
unlike 195
unresolved 163
update 180
updated 9-10, 145, 173, 205, 250, 259
updates 10, 71, 94, 195, 246
updating 191
upfront 236
upgrade 23, 111
upload 49, 229
uploading 54
uptime 99
useful 66, 72, 149, 195-196
usefully 12
UserID 160
usually 201
utility 169
utilize 54, 56, 71, 98
utilizing 65
validate 243
validated 29-30, 127, 153
Validation 243
valuable 7
values 152, 203
variables 39, 75, 222

variance   6, 152, 240-241
variances   151-152, 168, 240
variation   17, 28, 37, 40-41, 70
vendor 78, 86, 94-95, 105, 110, 174
vendors   93, 95-96, 103, 173
verified 10, 29-30, 127
verify   73, 182, 217, 243, 254
Version 246, 260
versions   27, 34
versus 87, 89, 229
vertically   74
vetting 148
viable 149
victim 23
viewpoint   256
viewpoints   256
vigorously   238
violations   148
virtual 69, 89, 110
vis-à-vis   199
visibility 28, 38
vision   115, 135
visits   174
visualize   122, 156
vmware   93
voices 130
voided 252
volatile 81
volatility   244
volume   241
Volumes   131
volunteer   245
vsphere   93
warrant   226
warranty   1, 184
weaknesses   137
weekly 126
wellbeing   223
whether   7
-which 193
willing 195-196
window   158
within   64, 117, 151, 155, 157, 169, 187, 203, 216, 219

without 1, 13, 141, 219, 255
worked 60, 98, 135, 235, 258
workforce 26
workgroup 253
working 50, 62, 100, 189, 199, 221, 258
workload 40, 84, 90, 99, 103-104, 107, 112, 119
workloads 26, 30, 38, 73, 77, 79, 83, 95, 117-118, 120-121
workplace 223
Worksheet 4, 169, 177
writing 11, 143
written 1, 191, 223, 225
youhave 155
yourself 190, 214